REBOOT

RENEW

REJOICE

God's Powerful Presence
in 1st & 2nd Chronicles

*Our God's powerful presence helps us to
reboot our lives, renew our commitment to
Him, and live a life of rejoicing as a result.*

MELANIE NEWTON

JOYFUL
WALK
BIBLE
STUDIES

We extend our heartfelt thanks to the many women who served as editors for the original study—Michelle Burns, Julia Gendron, Abby Germer, Nancy Stephenson, Connie Crowley, Marlo Brazeal, and Kim Newton. Without their help, we could not have completed this project in a timely manner.

For questions about the use of this study guide or for bulk orders, please email us at melanienewton.com/contact.

Melanie Newton is the author of "Graceful Beginnings" books for anyone new to the Bible and "Joyful Walk Bible Studies" for established Christians. Her mission is to help women learn to study the Bible for themselves and to grow their Bible-teaching skills to lead others.

Joyful Walk Bible Studies are grace-based studies for women of all ages. Each study guide follows the inductive method of Bible study (observation, interpretation, application) in a warm and inviting format.

We pray that you and your group will find *Renew Reboot Rejoice Bible Study* to be a resource that God will use to strengthen you in your faith walk with Him.

Christ-Focused • Grace-Based • Bible-Rich

JOYFUL WALK MINISTRIES
FLOWER MOUND, TX

MELANIE NEWTON

Melanie Newton is a Louisiana girl who made the choice to follow Jesus while attending LSU. She and her husband Ron married and moved to Texas for him to attend Dallas Theological Seminary. They stayed in Texas where Ron led a wilderness camping ministry for troubled youth for many years. Ron now helps corporations with their challenging employees and is the author of the top-rated business book, *No Jerks on the Job*.

Melanie jumped into raising three Texas-born children and serving in ministry to women at her church. Through the years, the Lord has given her opportunity to do Bible teaching and to write grace-based Bible studies for women that are now available from her website (melanienewton.com) and on Bible.org. *Graceful Beginnings* books are for anyone new to the Bible. *Joyful Walk Bible Studies* are for maturing Christians.

Melanie Newton loves to help women learn how to study the Bible for themselves. She also teaches online courses for women to grow their Bible-teaching skills to help others—all with the goal of getting to know Jesus more along the way. Her heart's desire is to encourage you to have a joyful relationship with Jesus Christ so you are willing to share that experience with others around you.

"Jesus took hold of me in 1972, and I've been on this great adventure ever since. My life is a gift of God, full of blessings in the midst of difficult challenges. The more I've learned and experienced God's absolutely amazing grace, the more I've discovered my faith walk to be a joyful one. I'm still seeking that joyful walk every day."

Melanie

OTHER BIBLE STUDIES BY MELANIE NEWTON

All books by *Joyful Walk Ministries* are available as paperbacks and printable / fillable pdfs as well as digital reader versions. Download our catalogue and get resources for your spiritual growth at melanienewton.com.

Graceful Beginnings books for anyone new to the Bible:

A Fresh Start (basics for new Christians)
Painting the Portrait of Jesus (the Gospel of John)
The God You Can Know (the character of God)
Grace Overflowing (an overview of Paul's 13 letters)
The Walk from Fear to Faith (7 Old Testament women)
Satisfied by His Love (women who knew Jesus)
Seek the Treasure (study of Ephesians)
Pathways to a Joyful Walk (6 pathways to a joy-filled life)
Songs of the Heart That Light My Way (selected Psalms)

Joyful Walk Bible Studies for growing Christians:

Adorn Yourself with Godliness (1 Timothy and Titus, also in Spanish)
Everyday Women, Ever Faithful God (Old Testament women, also in Spanish)
Connecting Faith to Life on Planet Earth (Genesis 1-11; Revelation)
Graceful Living (the essentials for a grace-based Christian life)
Graceful Living Today (a devotional journal for a joyful life)
Healthy Living (Colossians and Philemon)
Heartbreak to Hope (the Gospel of Mark)
Identity: Sticking to Your Faith in a Pull-Apart World (Ezra thru Malachi)
Knowing Jesus, Knowing Joy (Philippians, also in Spanish)
Live Out His Love (New Testament women)
Perspective (1and 2 Thessalonians)
Profiles of Perseverance (Old Testament men, also in Spanish)
Radical Acts (Acts)
Reboot, Renew, Rejoice (1 and 2 Chronicles)
The God-Dependent Woman (2 Corinthians)
To Be Found Faithful (2 Timothy)

Resources for leading others

Be a Christ-Focused Small Group Leader
Leap into Lifestyle Disciplemaking
Bible Study Leadership Made Easy
Painting the Picture of Jesus (the "I Am's" of Jesus lessons for children)
Teaching Children the God They Can Know (the character of God for children)

Contents

Using This Study Guide

This study guide consists of 11 lessons that cover two Old Testament books—1st and 2nd Chronicles. You will be reading through both books though not covering every detail. The lessons are divided into 5 daily sections (about 20 minutes in length). The first 4 sections contain a detail study of the passages. The last section is a podcast that provides additional insight to the lesson.

If you cannot do the entire lesson one week, please read the Bible passage covered by the lesson and try to do the "Day One Study" of the lesson.

THE BASIC STUDY

Each lesson includes core questions covering the passage narrative. These core questions will take you through the process of inductive Bible study—observation, interpretation, and application. The process is more easily understood in the context of answering these questions:

- What does the passage say? (Observation: what's actually there) These will help you to notice all the information that is given in the text.

- What does it mean? (Interpretation: the author's intended meaning)

- How does this apply to me today? *(Application: making it personal)* **Reboot, renew, rejoice** questions lead you to introspection and application of specific truths to your life.

STUDY ENHANCEMENTS

Deeper Discoveries (optional): Embedded within the sections are *optional* questions for research of subjects we don't have time to cover adequately in the lessons or contain information that significantly enhance the basic study. If you are meeting with a small group, your leader may give you the opportunity to share your "discoveries."

Study Aids: To aid in proper interpretation and application of the study, six additional study aids are located where appropriate in the lesson:

- Historical Insights

- Scriptural Insights

- From the Hebrew (definitions of Hebrew words)

- Focus on the Meaning

- Think About It (thoughtful reflection)

Other useful study tools: Use online tools or apps (blueletterbible.org or "Blue Letter Bible app" is especially helpful) to find *cross references* (verses with similar content to what you are studying) and meanings of the *original Hebrew words or phrases* used (usually called "interlinear"). You can also look at any verse in *various Bible translations* to help with understanding what it is saying.

PODCASTS

Find podcasts for these lessons at melanienewton.com/podcasts (choose "6: 1 & 2 Chronicles) and on most podcast providers. Use the QR code for quick access. Or you can read the blogs associated with the podcasts at melanienewton.com/blog. Choose 1 & 2 Chronicles category then scroll to find the title you want. Listen to the first podcast as an introduction to the study.

OLD TESTAMENT SUMMARY

About 1700 years after God created everything, He sent judgment on a rebellious race through a worldwide Flood. He later separated the nations with different languages and scattered them from Babel. Abraham, Isaac, and Jacob were founding fathers of the Hebrew people. Sold into slavery, Joseph became a powerful foreign leader paving the way for his relatives to move to Egypt. The Israelites grew in number for ~400 years in Egypt but became slaves of the Egyptian rulers. So God delivered them from bondage through Moses who took the people across the Red Sea and taught them God's Law at Mt. Sinai. Joshua led the Israelites into the Promised Land after a 40-year trek in the wilderness because of their unbelief.

During the transition toward monarchy, there were deliverer-rulers called "Judges," the last of whom was Samuel. The first three Hebrew kings—Saul, David, and Solomon—each ruled 40 years. Under Rehoboam, the Hebrew nation divided into northern and southern kingdoms, respectively called Israel and Judah. Prophets warned against worshipping the foreign god Baal. After the reign of 19 wicked kings in the north, Assyria conquered and scattered the northern kingdom. In the south, 20 kings ruled for ~350 years, until Babylon took the people into captivity for 70 years. Zerubbabel, Ezra, and Nehemiah led the Jews back into Jerusalem over a 100-year period. More than 400 "silent years" spanned the gap between Malachi and Matthew.

The 39 books in the Old Testament are divided into 4 main categories:

- "The Law" (Genesis - Deuteronomy)—the beginning of the nation of Israel as God's chosen people; God giving His Laws to the people that made them distinct from the rest of the nations.

- "History" (Joshua - Esther)—narratives that reveal what happened from the time the people entered the Promised Land right after Moses died until 400 years before Christ was born.

- "Poetry & Wisdom" (Job-Song of Solomon)—take place at the same time as the history books but are set apart because they are written as poems and have a lot of wise teaching in them.

- "Prophets" (Isaiah - Malachi)—concurrent with the books of history and, except for Lamentations, reflect the prophet's name through whom God spoke to the nation of Israel.

OLD TESTAMENT TIMELINE

The time period covered by this study is italicized in the chart below.

Historical Period	Years BC.	Leaders
The Patriarchs	2100 - 1800	Abraham, Isaac, Jacob
Israel in Egypt, Exodus, Conquest of Land	1800 - 1450	Moses, Joshua
Time of the Judges	1400 – 1050	Deborah, Gideon, Samuel
United Kingdom	*1050 – 930*	*Saul, David, Solomon*
Divided Kingdom—Judah	*930 – 586*	*Rehoboam, Asa, Jehoshaphat, Hezekiah, Josiah*
Restored Israel after Exile	538 – 400	*Zerubbabel*, Ezra, Nehemiah

In this study, you will learn how to live faithfully to God in the midst of even a corrupt culture. Political intrigue. Divided nation. Wicked leaders. Good leaders. Compromise that causes heartache. Renewed commitment needed to bring revival and rejoicing. Sounds like today, doesn't it? God knows exactly what we are going through today in your world because He's been through it before with Israel! And His solutions haven't changed. This study of 1 and 2 Chronicles will help Old Testament history come alive for you.

DISCUSSION GROUP GUIDELINES

Anyone can do this study alone. If you are doing this as part of a group, we suggest you use the following guidelines to maintain a safe environment for your group members to learn together.

1. **Attend consistently** whether your lesson is done or not. You'll learn from the other women, and they want to get to know you.

2. **Set aside time** to work through the study questions. The goal of Bible study is to **get to know** Jesus. He will change your life.

3. **Share your insights** from your personal study time. As you spend time in the Bible, Jesus will teach you truth through His Spirit inside you.

4. **Respect each other's insights**. Listen thoughtfully. Encourage each other as you interact. Refrain from dominating the discussion if you have a tendency to be talkative. ☺

5. **Celebrate our unity** in Christ. Avoid bringing up controversial subjects such as politics, divisive issues, and denominational differences.

6. **Maintain confidentiality.** Remember that anything shared during the group time is not to leave the **group** (unless permission is granted by the one sharing).

7. **Pray for one another** as sisters in Christ.

8. **Get to know the women** in your group. Please do not use your small group members for solicitation purposes for home businesses, though.

There is a small group discussion guide available at the end of this study. Anyone can use the guide to lead a group through a discussion of the questions in this study. This is especially useful for groups that have less than two hours to meet together.

Enjoy your Joyful Walk Bible Study!

Recommended: Listen to the podcast "A Fresh Start" as an introduction to the whole study. Use the following listener guide.

A Fresh Start

A FRESH START FOR ISRAEL—1948 AD

- In 70 AD, the Jews were forcibly exiled from their land in the Middle East by the Roman Empire. By the 1800s, fewer than 25,000 Jews lived in their ancient homeland.

- In the late 1800s, Jews began returning to re-establish themselves in their ancient homeland. They made deserts bloom and revived the almost dead Hebrew language. The horrors of World War II spurred a greater interest in supporting a national Israel.

- On May 14, 1948, the Jewish People's Council gathered in Tel Aviv and declared the establishment of the State of Israel. For the first time in 2000 years, the Jews once again had their own nation. It was the second reboot of Israel. The first reboot occurred 2500 years earlier in 537 BC.

REBOOT OF ISRAEL—537 BC

- The Jewish people descended from Abraham to whom God promised descendants, a specific area of land (Israel), and a blessing for the whole world through his descendant.

- After 700 years of living in their promised land, God determined that the Jewish people would be in a "70-year time out" from living in their land because of their evil behavior.

- At the end of the 70 years of exile, the Jews were allowed to return home and rebuild their Temple in Jerusalem. Many of them had little concept of living in the "promised land" and how to worship God there. They didn't know their identity or purpose for existence.

- God in His goodness inspired someone to chronicle the history of His people from their first calling through Abraham to what happened that caused the death of the nation and exile to Babylon. That's what we have in 1 and 2 Chronicles.

- Chronicles showed a despairing people that they had a powerful, faithful God who would strengthen them to rebuild the Temple and their nation. God gave them an opportunity to reboot their relationship with Him. The power of His presence was still there.

THE VALUE OF A REBOOT

A reboot is "an act or instance of making a change in order to establish a new beginning."

- God offers every human being a rebooted spiritual life through His gospel message. Trusting in Jesus Christ is the first reboot all humans need to have in their lives.

- Other types of reboots for believers:
  - ✓ Repentance of sinful behavior. Repentance means to change your mind about that behavior and choose obedience to God instead. Isaiah 1:16b-17a
  - ✓ Making changes of location, relationships, or lifestyle because of unhealthy situations.
- We can reboot because we have the power of God's presence with us to enable it. Then, we can choose to renew our commitment to God when enticed by the world.

RENEW YOUR COMMITMENT TO GOD

To renew means "to restore to freshness and vigor." Renew can also be a commitment to keep going in the same direction.

- Every day we have the opportunity to enjoy our relationship with God with renewed freshness and vigor.

- With every attack from the world, we must still choose to renew our commitment to God and not fold. The power of God's presence with us helps us to make that choice too. We are never without His guidance. *Isaiah 30:21*

REJOICE

- When you experience a reboot in your life or a sense of renewal in your daily relationship with God, our faithful God will fill your heart with His joy. Joy, rejoicing, gladness of heart, and singing are the outward expressions of what the Lord is doing in your heart.

- Today, we have a far greater reason to rejoice than the Jews did in 500 BC because the Messiah did come in the person of the Lord Jesus Christ.
  - ✓ Jesus was fully God and fully man. He showed us how to live as humans in relationship with God. He showed us how to live as humans in dependence on God.
  - ✓ Through His death on the cross, He paid the price for our sin, freeing us to be completely reconciled to God and adopted as His children.
  - ✓ Through His resurrection, Jesus released us from our death sentence as His Spirit comes to live inside us, completely regenerating our dead spirits.
  - ✓ All we need to do is to say yes to the invitation to commit our lives to the Lord Jesus Christ. That's the greatest reboot anyone can experience. That's His power at work in us. And it is permanent.

Our God's powerful presence helps us to reboot our lives, renew our commitment to Him, and live a life of rejoicing as a result. How have you experienced the power of His presence?

Let Jesus satisfy your heart with the power of His presence. Then, live in that power!

Israel's Heritage and First Kings

1 An Unbroken Connection

1 Chronicles 1-12 (2500-1010 BC)

DAY ONE STUDY

The ABCs of Chronicles—Author, Background, and Context

Like any book you read, it always helps to know a bit about the author, the background setting for the story (i.e., past, present, future), and where the book fits into a series (that's the context). The same is true of Bible books.

AUTHOR

Unlike most of the New Testament books, we often do not know the authors of the Old Testament books, especially the ones of history. Nothing in the text of the books of Chronicles tells us definitively of the author(s). The Babylonian Talmud (rabbinical writings) identifies Ezra, a priest and scribe who lived within 100 years of the exile, as the author. Most people refer to the unknown writer as "the Chronicler." Originally written as one book, Chronicles was likely finished around 450 to 425 BC because the last descendant of David listed in the genealogies lived at that time. According to many references within the books, the Chronicler used existing historical records.

BACKGROUND

Because of their sinful behavior, God determined that the Jewish people would be in a "time out" from living in their land. From 605 BC to 586 BC, the Jews were progressively removed from their homeland and taken into captivity in Babylon and other areas of the Babylonian Empire. For seventy years, they learned how to live in a pagan environment away from their Temple and their land.

In 539 BC, Babylon fell to the Persian monarch Cyrus the Great. Cyrus soon decreed that the Jewish people could return to Judea and rebuild their Temple in Jerusalem. Three groups of people returned over the next 100 years—the first led by Zerubbabel in 537 BC, the second led by Ezra 80 years later, and the third group came with Nehemiah 15 years after that.

The remnant returned to a ruined Jerusalem, a destroyed temple, and other obstacles to their success. Many of them who had been born in Babylon had little concept of living in the "promised land" and how to worship God there. They didn't know their identity or purpose for existence. So the writer of Chronicles traced the history of God's people from their first calling through Abraham to what happened that caused the death of the nation and subsequent exile to Babylon. He reminded the new generation that God had been their help in ages past. He emphasized the unconditional covenant God made with David to maintain a descendant as leader of the people.

The author of the Chronicles showed a despairing people that they had a powerful, faithful God who would strengthen them to rebuild the Temple and the city of Jerusalem. And more importantly, he emphasized how important it was to stay faithful in their worship of the God who called them to be His people and a light to the world. The hope was that they would never again fall into the worship of other "gods" besides their own covenant God.

CONTEXT

Chronicles is considered one of the 12 books of "history" in the Old Testament (Joshua through Esther). Originally, the books of Samuel, Kings, and Chronicles were single books. During the time of the Septuagint (Greek) translation of the Hebrew Old Testament (in 200 BC), the scribes divided those long books, making them easier for copyists and readers to handle. That's why we have 6 books of history of the kings of Israel rather than 3. The original title for Chronicles was "Things Omitted." How's that for a title of a book? When Jerome translated the Bible into Latin (~400 AD), he suggested the title should be "*chronicle* of the whole sacred history." That name stuck.

Although 1 and 2 Chronicles come after the books of 1 and 2 Kings in our Bible, the historical record within Chronicles is concurrent with and supplementary to that of the books of Samuel and Kings. The books of Kings contain more detail about the northern kingdom of Israel, but the Chronicles focus on the southern kingdom of Judah. Because of this, over half of the content of Chronicles is unique as it focuses mainly on the religious nature of the people and their leaders during the years of David and his descendants after him. The end of 2 Chronicles connects historically to the book of Ezra and continues through Nehemiah. The book of Esther takes place between the first group of exiles returning to Judea led by Zerubbabel in 537 BC and the second group led by Ezra 80 years later.

> **Scriptural Insight:** Why do we need the books of 1–2 Chronicles when we already have the history of 2 Samuel and 1–2 Kings? Just as the gospels of Matthew, Mark, Luke, and John each offer a different perspective on the life of Jesus, so the books of Chronicles present Israel's history with a purpose different than the other historical books. The books of 2 Samuel and 1–2 Kings reveal the monarchies of Israel and Judah—in particular the sins of the nations that resulted in the exile. But the books of Chronicles, written after the time of the exile, focus on those elements of history that God wanted the returning Jews to meditate upon: obedience that results in God's blessing, the priority of the Temple and priesthood, and the unconditional promises to the house of David. (Chuck Swindoll, *First Chronicles Overview,* insight.org)

1. What background information about the books of Chronicles really grabbed your attention?

> **Historical Insight:** Are you unfamiliar with the Old Testament? On page 2 of this book, we provided an Old Testament summary and a timeline that includes the 465 years covered by this study—from the middle of David's reign to the exile.

2. To help your perspective of time, name a few influential people in your country or in your family over the past 400 years and why they are memorable.

Respond to the Lord about what He's shown you today.

DAY TWO STUDY

Ask the Lord Jesus to speak to you through His Word. Tell Him that you are listening.

Reboot, Renew, Rejoice

REBOOT

> **Focus on the Meaning:** Chronicles is a reboot. It is not just the same old material; it has a new tone, a new message, new truth about God to communicate. (James Duguid, "Why Study the Books of 1-2 Chronicles?" www.crossway.org)

Throughout Chronicles, we will see the value of a reboot. If you own a computer or other digital device, then you probably know that restarting that computer or device is known as a reboot. It clears away the old stuff that was causing trouble and refreshes the operating system so that it works better.

The term "reboot" has expanded its usage into other areas of life. According to the dictionary, a reboot is "an act or instance of making a change in order to establish a new beginning."

That's what God offers to every human being on the planet through His gospel message. Trust in Christ for your salvation and begin anew in your relationship with God. A rebooted spiritual life removes all the sin that separated you from God and replaces it with forgiveness for all your sins, redemption from the control of sin in your life, and reconciliation with God so that you are completely loved and accepted by Him. That's the first reboot every human needs to have in their life.

3. From the following verses, what "reboot" takes place at salvation?

    • 2 Corinthians 5:17—

    • 1 Thessalonians 1:9—

    • Ephesians 2:1-6—

There are other types of rebooting in the daily life of a believer. Whenever we are going the wrong way, away from God, God calls us to repentance—to change our mind about that behavior and choose obedience to Him instead. Sometimes we must reboot because of an unhealthy situation. That may require a move, a change of relationships, and/or lifestyle because of health issues. We'll see examples of these in the books of Chronicles.

4. Here are some New Testament verses about lifestyle reboots. What do you learn about when and how to make those reboots?

    • 1 Corinthians 15:33-34—

- Ephesians 5:1-7—

- Titus 2:11-14—

RENEW

Rebooting is an important tool that God uses to get us going in the right direction with Him. But when you choose to stay faithful to Him when given the opportunity to go the world's way, that's actually a decision to renew your relationship with God.

The term "renew" can mean "to restore to freshness and vigor," as in renewing our strength through sleep. That applies to our spiritual life as well. Every day we have the opportunity to enjoy our relationship with God with renewed freshness and vigor. But to renew can also mean to continue as in maintaining an ongoing subscription or membership. It's a commitment to keep going in the same direction. We will see people renew their relationship with God as they stay firmly committed to Him rather than straying away.

5. Here are some New Testament verses about renewal. What do you learn that will keep you renewed and restored to freshness and vigor?

- Romans 12:1-2—

- Colossians 1:9-12—

- Colossians 3:15-17—

REJOICE

Both experiencing a reboot in your life and a sense of renewal in your daily relationship with God should lead you to rejoice. I think you know what rejoice means. Joy, rejoicing, gladness of heart, and singing are the outward expressions of what the Lord is doing in your heart. We will see this frequently in Chronicles—27 times—as a reboot or renewal of their hearts toward God results in rejoicing.

6. Here are some New Testament verses about rejoicing because of God working in someone's life to reboot or renew them. What do you learn?

- Luke 19:1-10 (the tax collector)—

- 2 Corinthians 7:9 (about someone who repents)—

- Acts 16:25-34 (the jailer)—

Our God's powerful presence helps us to reboot our lives, renew our commitment to Him, and live a life of rejoicing as a result. This is the theme for the whole study.

7. *Reboot, renew, rejoice:* What about you? God's not done writing your story.

- Do you need a reboot in your life?

- Maybe you don't need a reboot, but would you like to renew your relationship with God in a more committed way?

- What has God done in your life up to this point through a reboot or renewal that leads you to rejoice?

Respond to the Lord about what He's shown you today.

DAY THREE STUDY

Israel's identity, "Who are we?"

Have you ever done any research into your genealogy (ancestors)? I spent quite a bit of time on that several years ago. One of my favorite websites to use was Ancestry.com. It contained a wealth of information about my great-great grandparents and even included some tidbits beyond just names and birthdates of what their lives were like. I loved that! Knowing about them made them seem more real to me. I don't know about you, but I feel a connection to that great-great grandmother when I learn a little bit about her life. For those who were definitely Christians, I look forward to meeting them in heaven.

But I also learned to be cautious about some of the connections. I'd get so excited to see that so and so was the daughter or son of the governor of Bermuda, a Scottish lord, or an early American founder only to find out that someone added that connection to our family line recklessly. When I traced the descendants of those famous people, my ancestor was not any part of that list. Trying to stay accurate as I put all my research into a book for my family members, I only included what I could meticulously prove was true.

The first nine chapters of 1 Chronicles is the Old Testament Ancestry.com. The Chronicler meticulously researched and included the lineages of the twelve tribes of Israel so that those who were returning to their homeland after the exile would know where to go and find their land (1 Chronicles 9:2). David's descendants are listed several times to make sure everyone knew who was eligible to be king again. The restored nation needed priests who could prove they were from the tribe of Levi so they could serve at the rebuilt temple. No hearsay allowed.

The Jewish people trying to resettle their land and reboot their lives needed to know their identity. Who were they? Why were they a people? What was their purpose? They found the answers in Chronicles as they discovered their rich heritage and their unbroken connection with their God-ordained beginnings as a people. They could know the biographies of their ancestors and feel connected to them. Even more importantly, they needed to know who their God was and why they should only serve Him. They needed to see that He was a faithful God, and they could trust Him. Our God is the same God so we can learn about Him as well.

Let's get started

Ask the Lord Jesus to speak to you through His Word. Tell Him that you are listening.

Relax. We aren't going to ask you to read 1 Chronicles chapters 1-10. Whew! Those chapters contain a lot of names that don't matter so much to us (unless you are an avid student of history and love matching names found here with stories about those same people elsewhere in the Bible—feel free to do so). And the author jumped around a lot which can drive those of us who like order into utter frustration. But for the purpose of today's lesson, we are going to just look at key areas that help us understand the rest of the two books.

Appropriately, the beginning of 1 Chronicles starts with Adam, the first human created by God. Through his son, Seth, came the line of Noah and his three sons (vv. 1-27). From the descendants of Noah's son Shem, God chose Abraham to be the father of everyone thereafter known as Jews. Abraham's son Isaac had two sons, but God chose the second son Jacob to be the one from whom the 12 tribes of Israel would descend. Are you with me so far?

8. Look at 1 Chronicles 2:1. Read through these names of the 12 tribes of Israel. You will see them pop up in the narratives of Chronicles. Each tribe settled in its own section of the land. Consider that to be like states/provinces in a country. Where each tribe lived was pretty consistent for several hundred years, then things got jumbled up.

Since Levi's descendants were to be the religious leaders for all the tribes, they did not get one section of land. They were given designated plots throughout all the tribal areas. God took Joseph's two sons (Ephraim and Manasseh) and gave them each a tribal territory. There were still 12 tribal territories except Manasseh was huge, so it got 2 sections of land (east & west of the Jordan River).

> See the maps at the end of this study guide. Refer to these maps whenever you want to visualize the places being referenced in Chronicles.

9. Of those 12 tribes, Judah was the most important to the Chronicler because that was King David's tribe. So it comes next in the list (rest of chapter 2), including David's siblings and nephews. Then, David's descendants are listed in chapter 3.

   • Look at 1 Chronicles 3:1-9. Find **Solomon's** name in the list of David's sons.

   • Scan the names in vv. 10-16. Throughout this study, we'll be covering the lives and leadership of those kings (who are all David's heirs).

   • Notice that vv. 17-24 lists the royal line of David after the exile.

After listing more descendants of Judah who are not of David's line, chapters 4-8 cover the lineage of the other 11 tribes. Occasionally, place names are given to help them locate their homeland.

10. Because the tribe of Levi was chosen by God to be the source of religious leaders for Israel, chapter 6 is very detailed. The two divisions of this tribe were the priests and the Levites. These two groups are referenced frequently in Chronicles. Read 1 Chronicles 6:48-49. What were the duties of each group?

Chapter 9 continues the emphasis on the priests and Levites but focuses on those who returned from exile. Only those who descended from Aaron, Moses' brother, could be priests at the Temple. The group called "the Levites" were like local pastors for communities as well as servants for all aspects of the Tabernacle and Temple including security (gatekeepers) and leading worship. In order to reestablish worship of God in the land, those who returned from exile had to prove their lineage in order to serve in either capacity.

> **Focus on the Meaning:** That proving of one's ancestry reminds me of joining the Daughters of the American Revolution. In order to be accepted into this prestigious organization, one must have written documentation to prove that an ancestor served in the American Revolutionary War (1776-1783) either as a soldier or civilian that provided resources for the soldiers.

Israel's first king, Saul (from the tribe of Benjamin), is highlighted briefly in 1 Chronicles 9:35-10:14. He disobeyed God over and over again. So God ripped the kingdom away and gave it to David. The end of chapter 10 transitions the reader to David—Israel's second, and greatest, king—who is the central person of the rest of 1 Chronicles.

11. Thrown in the midst of the endless sea of names in 1 Chronicles 1-9 are tidbits about a few of the common people.

    But the noble make noble plans, and by noble deeds they stand. (Isaiah 32:8)

    - To make my reading through these passages more interesting, I highlighted every woman mentioned. There are more than 50 women listed by name as distinctive mothers, sisters, wives, and daughters. One woman was particularly interesting to me. Read 1 Chronicles 7:24. What is said about Sheerah from the tribe of Ephraim?

    Focus on the Meaning: The two Beth-horons were apparently Canaanite towns that the Israelites captured and destroyed in the conquest under Joshua. "Built" may mean rebuilt, or restored, or fortified. Two of the three cities, Lower Beth-Horon and Upper Beth-Horon were on a hillside, one high above the other. These works were done either by her design or by her instigation and influence upon those who did the building. Either way, Sheerah made an impact on her time and community that was remembered hundreds of years later!

    - Years ago, a book about "the prayer of Jabez" swept the Christian community. Here's the source. Read 1 Chronicles 4:9-10. What do you learn about Jabez?

12. ***Reboot, renew, rejoice:*** Identity is essential to any reboot. Start with viewing yourself rightly.

    - If you have trusted in Jesus Christ for your salvation, the Bible says that you are "in Christ." That is your identity. Being in Christ means that you are also adopted into God's family as His child. You are one of God's saints, totally loved and accepted by Him because of your faith in Jesus Christ. Your purpose is to love God with all that you are and to make disciples for Christ through your words and actions. This brings glory to God and reasons to rejoice.

    - If you have not trusted in Jesus Christ for your salvation, you can do that right now. God will reboot your life as you join His family as one who is "in Christ." All those things written above will now be true for you. Will you say yes to trusting in Jesus?

Respond to the Lord about what He's shown you today.

DAY FOUR STUDY

Historical Perspective

If you have ever been to Sunday school as a child, you likely know the story of David the young shepherd boy who slew the giant Goliath with a simple slingshot and one stone. We know that this brave shepherd boy grew up to be a great king of Israel. We also know that Jesus Christ descended from the house of David. Who was this David, and what can we learn from him?

In our Bibles, more has been written about David (66 chapters) than any other character in the Old Testament. In the New Testament, there are fifty-nine references to this great man. We not only can read about David's life in 1 and 2 Samuel, 1 Kings, and 1 Chronicles, we can glean insight into what he thought and felt by reading many of the psalms he wrote (73 are attributed to David).

In Hebrew, the name David means "beloved." David is the only person in the Bible whose scriptural epitaph reads "a man after God's own heart" (1 Samuel 13:14; Acts 13:22). God said this about him before he did anything great. He was just a young teen faithfully doing the chores related to family life (caring for the family flock). David was born in 1040 BC and is described as handsome and ruddy with beautiful eyes. As a teen, he was anointed by the prophet Samuel to be God's chosen king. From that day, the Holy Spirit remained with him for the rest of his life.

Since the purpose of the book of Chronicles is the reboot of Israel as a people who worship God, the Chronicler focused on David's life example.

Read 1 Chronicles 11:1-9. Ask the Lord Jesus to speak to you through His Word. Tell Him that you are listening.

13. After Saul's death, God had told David to settle at Hebron with all the people who had been with him (2 Samuel 2:1). The tribe of Judah made David king right away. It took more than 7 years for the rest of the tribes to confirm it for themselves in 1010 BC. How did that happen (vv. 2-4)?

14. Every nation needs a capital city. What did David do in vv. 4-9?

Historical Insight: Jerusalem was a natural fortress because of its location on a rise surrounded on three sides by deep valleys. The site was a noteworthy place in Israel's history from the time of Abraham when he gave a tithe to Melchizedek, the king of Salem (Genesis 14:18). The Jebusites were Canaanites. It was located on the border between Judah and Benjamin but was controlled by neither tribe. Locating his royal city in a newly conquered town that wasn't attached to any particular tribe helped David to unite the kingdom under his rule without seeming to subordinate one tribe to the others. The city covered about 12 acres and became known as Zion, the City of David. (*NIV Study Bible 1985 Edition,* note on 2 Samuel 5:6-7, pp. 429-430)

15. Skim through 1 Chronicles 11:10-25, The title given to this section in my Bible is "David's Mighty Men." I love that title! They were strong warriors who took their stand in the middle of the fray and defended their territory to bring victory. God sent those men to David (1 Samuel 22:1-2). Note: Joab, Abishai, and Asahel were David's nephews.

- What grabs your attention about these men?

- Scan vv. 26-47. Notice the diversity.

16. In 1 Chronicles 12, we read more about those who came to align themselves with David from the other tribes when David had been on the run hiding from Saul. *"Day after day men came to help David, until he had a great army, like the army of God" (1 Chronicles 12:22).* Scan 1 Chronicles 12 to see how God provided the strong support of friends to David. What grabs your attention about these men?

17. What encouraging message did God give to David in 1 Chronicles 12:18?

18. How did David celebrate with his friends and allies when he became king (1 Chronicles 12:38-40)?

> **Scriptural Insight:** The Chronicler presented David as a strong model king by selecting four pictures from his life: 1) his crowning (showing God's choice of him); 2) his capture of Jerusalem (the victory that led to the building of the Temple later); 3) his mighty men (showing the attraction of his personal character); and 4) the gathering of multitudes behind his leadership, showing his influence on the masses. (*Dr. Constable's Notes on 1 Chronicles 2019 Edition,* p. 9)

19. ***Reboot, renew, rejoice:*** We all need someone to have our backs. God does have our backs already as He goes before us, behind us, and all around us (Psalm 139). And He uses people to do that work for Him. If you are surrounded by godly people whom God sends to surround you, that is in a sense being supported by the army of God. I've seen this happen at a women's retreat. Women who were hurting and needing fresh support, even coming to the retreat alone and feeling alone beforehand, were completely surrounded by a whole army of

women who said, "We are with you!" The lonely began feeling supported by God's army of women. What a great feeling to have that kind of support!

- When have you been surrounded with those who have given you strong support like David's "Mighty Men" did for him? Describe what happened.

- How do you show appreciation to those whom God has given to support you?

- If you are needing support right now, but don't have it, ask the Lord to do so for you.

REBOOT RENEW REJOICE

20. What is your one take-away from Lesson 1?

Our God's powerful presence helps us to reboot our lives, renew our commitment to Him, and live a life of rejoicing as a result.

Respond to the Lord about what He's shown you today.

Recommended: Listen to the podcast "Knowing Who You Are" after doing this lesson to reinforce what you have learned. Use the following listener guide.

Knowing Who You Are

"Look to the rock from which you were cut and to the quarry from which you were hewn…" (Isaiah 51:1)

FEELING CONNECTED

Feeling like you belong to a story that began before you—and unfolds with you—helps to shape your perspective and purpose. In fact, this is the appeal of businesses that sell genealogical information. They market testimonies of excited clients claiming "Now I know who I am!" It's the power of feeling connected. (Randy Guliuzza, *Acts & Facts*, December 2019, p. 17)

- When we believe in the Lord Jesus as Savior, we become members of a new family with a rich history beginning with true royalty—the Lord Jesus who descended from David.

- The first nine chapters of 1 Chronicles is the Old Testament Ancestry.com. The Jewish people trying to resettle their land and reboot their lives needed to know their identity. Who were they? Why were they a people? What was their purpose?

- They found the answers in Chronicles as they discovered their rich heritage and their unbroken connection with their God-ordained beginnings as a people.

BEING A MEMORABLE WOMAN

- In the first 9 chapters of 1 Chronicles, there are 53 references to women listed by name as distinctive mothers, sisters, wives, and daughters. To be mentioned specifically in the historical record meant you were someone or did something that was memorable. *Isaiah 32:8*

- As a descendant of Joseph's son Ephraim, Sheerah is credited with rebuilding three towns on the edge of Ephraim's allotted territory in Israel after it was conquered. She made an impact on her time and her community that was remembered hundreds of years later. The Holy Spirit made sure her name was in there.

  "His daughter was Sheerah, who built Lower and Upper Beth Horon as well as Uzzen Sheerah." (1 Chronicles 7:24)

- Memorable women who knew their identity as a worshiper of the God of Israel were part of the nation's heritage.

KNOWING WHO YOU ARE

- In our world, identity drives everything about life.

- Knowing our spiritual identity is even more important.

- Have you trusted in Jesus Christ for your salvation? If so, you received a new spiritual identity from that very moment you said yes to believing in Jesus.

- Every Christian is a new creation with a new identity in Christ. This new identity declares how God, who is our authority, now views you. It is what He has done for us and to us that really counts, not what the culture thinks of us or what we think of ourselves. And there are wonderful perks that go along with this new position in life.

- Your faith in Jesus Christ sets you free from your previous sin-stained existence to enjoy a new life. But your ability to live out this freedom depends upon your understanding of who you now are.

- How we see ourselves directs how we live our faith walk. That was true for the Jews returning to Israel in 500 BC. That is true today. For us as Christians, we need to grasp the FACT that every believer gets a **new life** with a **radical** new identity—something we never had before, and something no one before Jesus' resurrection ever had!! And this new identity sets us free to live a radically new kind of life—a joyful life experiencing the power of God's presence.

- The moment we believe, the old self that was born **in Adam** died. A new self with the same body but a new interior started life as a new person with a new nature and a new inheritance. That's your reboot. The Holy Spirit places you in the Body of Christ. You are united with Christ. And Christ comes to live in you as His Spirit permanently indwells you and establishes changes in your relationship with God that are mind-blowingly wonderful. The power of God's presence is in you and with you forever! This radical new identity means you can never go back to not being **in Christ.** Ever!

- One of the fundamental questions of the human race is that of identity. People ask, "Who am I?" The one secure, eternal answer is that through faith in Jesus Christ you can say this,

"I am in Christ, a child of God, one of God's saints, totally loved and accepted by God."

That's who you are because of the power of God's presence in you. It's an identity that no circumstance can change!

Let Jesus satisfy your heart with the power of His presence. Then, live in that power!

David

2 Rejoice in All Things

1 Chronicles 13-21 (1010-970 BC)

DAY ONE STUDY

Things to note when studying the Old Testament

The books of the Old Testament (except for Genesis and Job) are the accounts of people living under the Old Covenant, the Law of Moses. It is important to keep that background and context in mind when studying them. For example:

- "Salvation" (especially in the Psalms) usually refers to a temporal *deliverance* from trouble or danger. It does not usually refer to eternal life.

- "The Holy Spirit" came upon certain individuals *temporarily* to empower them for special service (such as artisans, prophets, or kings) then left when that service was completed.

- "Forgiveness of sins" under the Law was accomplished through *atonement*, which means a "covering" for sin. A gracious God offered forgiveness to those who trusted in His lovingkindness, but it was at best *temporary* and *up-to-date*. The sacrifices in the Law of Moses did not provide someone forgiveness for tomorrow's sins.

Throughout the Old Testament, God's grace accepted any person who came to Him by faith. They received eternal salvation by their faith alone. That is consistent with what the New Testament teaches.

God's method of *managing* His people, however, was different, so *how* one's faith was expressed and lived out differed as well. The Tabernacle and the Temple represented the presence of God dwelling among His chosen people, Israel. There, the priests represented the people to God, and sacrificial offerings were the prime way to publicly express worship, repentance, and thanksgiving. God wanted the worshiper's *heart* first. Where one's *heart* was right, sacrifices could be acceptable to God as an expression of inner faith. While we no longer express worship to God through animal sacrifices, He still desires the hearts of His people above all else.

When Jesus Christ died on the cross, He brought to a close the age of the Old Covenant (the Law of Moses) and simultaneously inaugurated the New Covenant in which we live. So as we read these Old Testament books, we will read first to obtain accurate understanding of what the author(s) meant. Then, we will use New Testament teachings to apply truth about God to your everyday life in Jesus Christ.

One more thing: Much of Chronicles is narrative. That means the text describes what happened. It is descriptive, not prescriptive.

- *Descriptive* = observation of what actually happened, how people lived and made choices on how to do life at the time.

- *Prescriptive* = command from God about how to live or do something that applies to all believers, all people groups, and all time periods.

So we can't take these passages in Chronicles and create a formula for doing things a certain way to guarantee God's blessing on the result.

Read 1 Chronicles 13:1-14. Ask the Lord Jesus to speak to you through His Word. Tell Him that you are listening.

1. ***Deeper Discoveries (optional):*** Do some research about the ark of the Covenant (also called the ark of the testimony or the ark of God). What was it? What did it look like? What was its purpose? Where was it supposed to be kept?

> **Historical Insight:** About seventy years earlier (1 Samuel 4-6), the Philistines were beating the Israelites badly in a battle. The Israelite commander thought the answer was to bring the ark to the battlefield from Shiloh (where it had been properly sitting inside the Tabernacle). The Philistines captured the ark and brought it to their territory. Since the ark represented God's holy presence with Israel, God made life miserable for the Philistines until they returned it back to Israel. The Philistines put it in a new cart with newly yoked cows (the Philistine way to please their gods) to return the ark to an Israelite border town. It was eventually moved to the home of Abinadab (a Levite) in Kiriath Jearim where his son Eleazar was put in charge of guarding the ark.

2. What did David desire to do (vv. 1-3)?

3. Let's talk about what happened.

   • How was the ark supposed to be moved? See Exodus 25:12-15 and Numbers 4:15.

   • Why did God get angry at Uzzah?

   • What was David's response (vv. 11-13)?

   • Why do you think he responded with anger at first?

- What did God do for Obed-Edom? Note: Remember this man because his name comes up repeatedly in 1 Chronicles.

Think About It: Before anyone gets mad about this, Uzzah knew better. His father was Abinadab (2 Samuel 6:3) who had carefully housed the ark for many years! Uzzah's older brother Eleazar had been the guardian of the ark, keeping everyone away from it. Can you imagine that responsibility? Had familiarity removed the sense of awe that the ark deserved? Were they thinking of the ark as a piece of furniture representing God rather than God's holiness Himself?

Read 1 Chronicles 14:1-3, 8-17.

Historical Insight: Hiram, the Phoenician king of Tyre (modern Lebanon), was the first to accord the newly established King David international recognition. It was vital to him to have good relations with the king of Israel since Israel dominated the inland trade routes to Tyre, and Tyre was dependent on Israelite agriculture for much of its food. (*NIV Study Bible 1985 Edition*, note on 2 Samuel 5:11, p. 430)

4. The pesky Philistines were back. They had been Israel's nemesis for about 100 years.

- What did David do before responding to the attack? See also 1 Samuel 23:1-6.

- What grabbed your attention in vv. 8-17?

5. Compare how David approached fighting battles with how he approached moving the ark. What had David failed to do with the more important task of moving the ark? See also 1 Chronicles 15:13.

6. ***Reboot, renew, rejoice:*** David put Uzzah in a dangerous position by using the world's method (mixed with superstition) to do something "honorable," while leading a large praise and worship time as he did it. So he thought God would be pleased. Uzzah became the bad example of how not to treat God and His holiness. We do the same thing today. Think about this as you answer the following questions:

- How often do you take something from your culture that seems to provide a good solution to your challenges in life (parenting, marriage, surviving in a workplace, relationships, finances, sinful behavior) and think that the logical outcome will be pleasing to God even if the steps you follow are not in agreement with what God says in His Word?

- God gives clear directions on how to approach life His way rather than the world's way. It's our responsibility to inquire of Him through the written word accessible to everyone. Ask the Lord Jesus to give you clear direction in His Word on how to meet that life challenge in a God-honoring way rather than the world's way.

Think About It: Participation in praise and worship of God, even enthusiastically, does not compensate for deliberate disobedience.

Respond to the Lord about what He's shown you today.

DAY TWO STUDY

Read 1 Chronicles 15:1-16:3. Ask the Lord Jesus to speak to you through His Word. Tell Him that you are listening.

Did you wonder (as I did while reading this passage) why David didn't just go ahead and move the Tabernacle to Jerusalem and use that to house the ark of the Lord in its designated spot, the Most Holy Place? While pondering that, I was reminded how big that Tabernacle area was. Perhaps there wasn't room in Jerusalem yet for it. Or it could be that the Tabernacle was pretty fragile by this time and could not easily survive a move. Then, why bring the ark to Jerusalem instead of returning it to the Tabernacle at Gibeon? David perhaps wanted to protect it and make sure it would not be misused again and captured by an enemy army. If he asked God about this, we don't have a record of it. God wasn't displeased by moving the ark to Jerusalem, though. After all, as God, He could be present in both places at once!

7. David pitched a special tent to house the ark in Jerusalem. It was time to move it—again! What had he learned since the last attempt to move the ark (vv. 1-13)?

8. Besides the Levites who were carrying the ark, who else accompanied David and what were they doing (vv. 16-26)?

9. Describe the scene in 15:27-16:3 as though you were there to watch.

10. **Deeper Discoveries (optional):** Read Psalm 68. David wrote this about bringing the ark to its resting place in Jerusalem. Notice all the references to rejoicing and singing.

Read 1 Chronicles 16:4-6; 37-42.

11. The ark was now accessible in Jerusalem.

- What new activities did David start in Jerusalem on a regular basis?

- What remained the same (vv. 39-40)? Why?

Scriptural Insight: The Tabernacle remained at Gibeon until Solomon's construction of the Temple in Jerusalem, when it was stored within the Temple. The existence of these two shrines—the Tabernacle and the temporary structure for the ark in Jerusalem—accounts for the two high priests: Zadok serving in Gibeon and Abiathar in Jerusalem. (*NIV Study Bible 1985 Edition,* note on 1 Chronicles 16:39, p. 607)

The words in 1 Chronicles 16:7-36 are also found in Psalm 105, 96, and 106. Many of them are found in parts of other psalms. David used words he had written before this time that meant so much to him already and combined them to fit the occasion. We see this often in Psalms where phrases and whole sections of one psalm are repeated in several others. The familiarity of words helps with worship as they flow easily from the heart and mind.

As you read 1 Chronicles 16:7-36, mark anything that grabs your attention about God and the reasons we should praise Him.

16 *⁷ That day David first appointed Asaph and his associates to give praise to the LORD in this manner: ⁸ Give praise to the LORD , proclaim his name; make known among the nations what he has done ⁹ Sing to him, sing praise to him; tell of all his wonderful acts. ¹⁰ Glory in his holy name; let the hearts of those who seek the LORD rejoice. ¹¹ Look to the LORD and his strength; seek his face always. ¹² Remember the wonders he has done, his miracles, and the judgments he pronounced, ¹³ you his servants, the descendants of Israel, his chosen ones, the children of Jacob. ¹⁴ He is the LORD our God; his judgments are in all the earth. ¹⁵ He remembers his covenant forever, the promise he made, for a thousand generations, ¹⁶ the covenant he made with Abraham, the oath he swore to Isaac. ¹⁷ He confirmed it to Jacob as a decree, to Israel as an everlasting covenant: ¹⁸ "To you I will give the land of Canaan as the portion you will inherit." ¹⁹ When they were but few in number, few indeed, and strangers in it, ²⁰ they wandered from nation to nation, from one kingdom to another. ²¹ He allowed no one to oppress them; for their sake he rebuked kings: ²² "Do not touch my anointed ones; do my prophets no harm."*

²³ Sing to the Lord, all the earth; proclaim his salvation day after day. ²⁴ Declare his glory among the nations, his marvelous deeds among all peoples. ²⁵ For great is the LORD and most worthy of praise; he is to be feared above all gods. ²⁶ For all the gods of the nations are idols, but the LORD made the heavens. ²⁷ Splendor and majesty are before him; strength and joy are in his dwelling place. ²⁸ Ascribe to the LORD , all you families of nations, ascribe to the LORD glory and strength. ²⁹ Ascribe to the LORD the glory due his name; bring an offering and come before him. Worship the LORD in the splendor of his holiness. ³⁰ Tremble before him, all the earth! The world is firmly established; it cannot be moved. ³¹ Let the heavens rejoice, let the earth be glad; let them say among the nations, "The LORD reigns!" ³² Let the sea resound, and all that is in it; let the fields be jubilant, and everything in them! ³³ Let the trees of the forest sing, let them sing for joy before the LORD , for he comes to judge the earth.

³⁴ Give thanks to the LORD , for he is good; his love endures forever. ³⁵ Cry out, "Save us, God our Savior; gather us and deliver us from the nations, that we may give thanks to your holy name, and glory in your praise." ³⁶ Praise be to the LORD , the God of Israel, from everlasting to everlasting.

12. What grabs your attention about God and the reasons we should praise Him?

- In vv. 8-22—

- In vv. 23-33—

- In vv. 34-36—

Focus on the Meaning: These Old Testament people knew God by the personal name *Yahweh.* In our English translations, it is often written as LORD in capital letters. In the Old Testament, you'll find the phrase "the LORD your God" or "the LORD our God" at least 500 times. Every time, that phrase is emphasizing, "We have a personal God. His name is *Yahweh.*" It's the name by which God wished to be known and worshiped in Israel and by Israel. *Yahweh* means, "I am." This name expressed His character as constant, dependable and faithful. Several times in the gospels, Jesus applied God's name "I am" to Himself (John 4:26; 8:58). So the ever-faithful, promise-keeping God of the Old Testament is embodied in the Lord Jesus Christ of the New Testament and forever. We still have a personal God. As Bible teacher Tony Evans says, "Jesus is God's selfie!"

13. ***Reboot, renew, rejoice:*** Use any creative means (poem, prose, song, art, craft) to respond to the Lord in praise and worship as David did.

DAY THREE STUDY

Read 1 Chronicles 17:1-15. Ask the Lord Jesus to speak to you through His Word. Tell Him that you are listening.

14. According to v. 1, what was David's desire now? Review 1 Chronicles 15:1 and 16:1.

15. David did the right thing by consulting with God's prophet Nathan. Nathan thought it was a good idea. God answered both of them that night.

- What does God say in vv. 4-6?

- How has God been active in David's life (vv. 7-10)?

- What is God's promise about "building a house" (vv. 11-15)?

Scriptural Insight: The main reason God did not allow David to proceed with his plans to build Him a house (temple) was that God, not David, was sovereign. A secondary reason was that David was a man of war (22:8; 28:3). God reserved the right to choose who should build such a place, as well as when and where he should build it. It was inappropriate for David to decide these things, though his desire to honor God in this way was certainly commendable. *(Dr. Constable's Notes on 1 Chronicles 2019 Edition,* p. 44)

Read 1 Chronicles 17:16-27.

16. Discuss what David did and said in response to the revelation given.

Think About It: David followed God's message with a time of humble praise and thanksgiving to God. He wasn't mad at God but accepted God's sovereign decision as he should. God is God. Likewise, as His servants, we must trust His goodness in whatever He chooses to do even if our requests seem like such good and God-honoring things to do.

17. In 1 Chronicles 18, we can read of David's military victories that brought about peace for Israel that God promised (1 Chronicles 17:9-10). "The Lord gave David victory wherever he went (1 Chronicles 18:6,13)." Read 1 Chronicles 18:6-11. As a result of the victories, what did David accumulate, and what did he do with all that treasure?

18. *Reboot, renew, rejoice:*

- If you've asked God for something that you thought was such a good and God-honoring thing only to get a "No" answer from Him, how did you respond? What can you learn from David about the proper response in such a case?

- If God allowed someone else to do what you wanted to do but couldn't, what have you done to support that person's work?

Respond to the Lord about what He's shown you today.

DAY FOUR STUDY

In 1 Chronicles chapters 19 and 20, we learn that David and his army defeated the Ammonites, the Arameans, and the Philistines, including a couple of Goliath's relatives (20:5-7). In the process, he got a bejeweled crown, lots more plunder, and a labor force conscripted from the conquered peoples to use for building projects. Each victory brought more riches to the King, the national coffers, and the Lord's work. God had forgiven his adultery with Bathsheba and murder of Uriah (2 Samuel 11 & 12) as David humbled himself and renewed his relationship with God. So the Chronicler could rightly say, *"David reigned over all Israel, doing what was just and right for all his people (1 Chronicles 18:14)."* Well, except for what happened in chapter 21.

Read 1 Chronicles 21:1-22:1. Ask the Lord Jesus to speak to you through His Word. Tell Him that you are listening.

Scratching your head as to why the census was so evil? Me too. There is some missing information here, no doubt. The adversary mentioned in 21:1 may have been a foreign enemy incited by Satan to threaten Israel. Best guesses are that the census-taking was due to David's pride in his army and their exploits, forgetting that God was the one who gave victory. It seems out of character, though, especially because David was so resistant to being talked out of it. Why he didn't inquire of the Lord first we don't know!

Regardless of the reasons, the Chronicler spends a lot of time on this for one main reason. It answers the question every Jewish man, woman, boy, or girl might ask when they return home from their time of exile, and someone insists they need to rebuild the Temple—right there on that pile of rubble. The question is, "Why must the Temple be **there**?"

19. What happened in vv. 1-7?

20. God wasn't pleased with David. David agreed with God. That's confession. So what happened next (vv. 8-14)?

Focus on the Meaning: Joab did the passive-aggressive thing by not counting 2 of the tribes in the numbering (v. 6). But the people of Israel suffered because of David's sin. That was no laughing matter. Thousands of those counted men died. It is amazing how many seemingly innocent people can be affected by one person's very public sin! Notice that this is the only place in the Bible where God offered someone a choice of punishment.

21. As the angel of death was about to hit Jerusalem, what happened (vv. 15-19)?

22. Describe the scene in vv. 20-27.

23. Based on vv. 18 and 26, what did David perceive about God's preference for the location of the future Temple (vv. 28-22:1)?

Scriptural Insight: The threshing floor of Araunah was located on Mount Moriah, immediately north of David's city and overlooking it. It was the place where God led Abraham to sacrifice his son Isaac (Genesis 22). Then, God intervened and spared Isaac's life by providing a ram instead. This is the place where we find the first mention of "worship" in the Bible (Genesis 22:5).

Fire from heaven to light the altar? I thought that only happened in the time of Elijah on Mt. Carmel (1 Kings 18). No, it happened here years before Elijah. God used fire from heaven to make a statement for sure! As a result, David declared that site would be the location for the Temple. God worked something good out of something awful. He does that from His grace. God spared Jerusalem and gave David and anyone else watching a sign from heaven that they could not ignore (angel with drawn sword and fire from heaven lighting up the altar)! The Gentile Araunah and his 4 sons got to see the God of Israel in action and received unexpected payment from a God-honoring King for their land that he could have taken from them for nothing. That's our God!

24. ***Reboot, renew, rejoice:*** Think about the things God has done to get your attention. What has He done to show you that He is Lord of your life as well as Lord of the people around you?

REBOOT RENEW REJOICE

25. What is your one take-away from Lesson 2?

Our God's powerful presence helps us to reboot our lives, renew our commitment to Him, and live a life of rejoicing as a result.

Respond to the Lord about what He's shown you today.

Recommended: Listen to the podcast "The Rewards of Approaching Life God's Way" after doing this lesson to reinforce what you have learned. Use the following listener guide.

The Rewards of Approaching Life God's Way

BETTER TO DO IT GOD'S WAY THE FIRST TIME!

- After King David got settled in Jerusalem, he thought it would be God's will to move the Ark of God from a western farming community to Jerusalem.

- Instead of using the method prescribed in the Law, David copied how the Philistines returned the captured Ark back to Israel—using a new cart pulled by newly yoked cows. When the oxen stumbled, Uzzah touched the Ark and died.

- David let a seemingly good idea from a surrounding culture influence him to supposedly "please" God by doing the same thing. Uzzah became the bad example of how not to treat God and His holiness.

- David consulted God's Word and made sure the priests and Levites did everything right "in accordance with the word of the Lord as they successfully moved the Ark to the tent inside Jerusalem. *1 Chronicles 15:13*

- They approached this task God's way rather than the world's way.

PRAISES, PRAYERS, AND PROMISES

- After David moved the Ark to Jerusalem, settling it in its own tent, David appointed a prayer team and orchestra to appear daily before the Lord. *1 Chronicles 16:4*

- David's psalm in 1 Chronicles chapter 16 is a beautiful combination of praise for how God brought the nation of Israel together to be His very own people plus praise for who He is and thanksgiving for what He has done.

- When David expressed his desire to build a temple for God in Jerusalem, God's answer was, "No. Then, God made several wonderful promises to David. David accepted God's sovereign decision. *1 Chronicles 17:26*

- David submitted to God's way. He didn't force the issue and go ahead and build the Temple just because he could. He approached life God's way and was rewarded for it with a promise of future heirs. He had not asked for that. God's grace gave Him that gift and rewarded David for his obedience.

- The Bible says the Lord gave David victory everywhere he went. In each victory, David gained treasure and labor—resources that could be used for the future Temple building.

A Prideful Decision with Unexpected Results

- In taking the census, David did not approach his authority as king according to God's ways. Many people died because of his prideful decision. David mourned his sin and pleaded with the Lord to spare the people of Israel and punish him instead.

- God sent a prophet to tell David to go to the threshing floor of a man named Araunah and build an altar. This spot just "happened" to be on Mount Moriah where Abraham had taken Isaac to sacrifice to God (Genesis 22:1-2).

  "[David] called on the Lord, and the Lord answered him with fire from heaven on the altar of burnt offering. Then the Lord spoke to the angel, and he put his sword back into its sheath (1 Chronicles 21:26-27)."

- God is the one who chose that site to be the location for His Temple. God worked something good out of something awful. He does that from His grace. God spared Jerusalem, giving David and anyone else watching a sign from heaven that they could not ignore—the angel with drawn sword and fire from heaven lighting up the altar!

- Araunah, who was a Gentile (not a Jew), and his sons got to see the God of Israel in action and received unexpected payment from a God-honoring King for their land that he could have taken from them for nothing. That's God's grace too.

Rejecting the Power of God's Presence with Us

- The incidents about the moving of the ark and taking the census show the problems we cause for ourselves and others around us when we reject approaching life God's way and choose to use the world's way or our own way instead. When we do that, we reject the power of God's presence with us.

- How often do we take something from our culture that seems to provide a good solution to our challenges in life and think that the logical outcome will be pleasing to God even if the choices we make are not in agreement with what God says in His Word? Think about the areas of parenting, marriage, surviving in a workplace, relationships, and recreational pleasures. God gives clear directions on how to approach life His way rather than the world's way. It's our responsibility to inquire of Him through the written word accessible to everyone. That's the Bible. What is written in 1 Chronicles is a great reminder to us.

Our God's powerful presence helps us to reboot our lives, renew our commitment to Him, and live a life of rejoicing as a result. Accessing and submitting to the power of God's presence in our lives makes a huge difference for us and for those we love.

Let Jesus satisfy your heart with the power of His presence. Then, live in that power!

David

3 The Joy of Delighting in God

1 Chronicles 22-29 (1010-970 BC)

DAY ONE STUDY

Historical Perspective

The books of 1 and 2 Chronicles focus on the line of the kings of Judah rather than those of the northern kingdom (also called Israel). David was the first king from Judah, and his descendants continued on the throne for generations. No other family took possession of the throne so that by the time of Jesus, any legitimate king would still be considered to have descended from David. When the nation was disciplined by God and fragmented, the stories of David and Solomon found in Chronicles were meant to encourage them to come back together to be God's people again, set apart for His purposes. God used the Chronicler to cast a vision of how to live in a renewed, blessed relationship with Himself.

David was made king over all of Israel 20 years after he was taken out of the sheep pastures and anointed by Samuel (1 Samuel 16:12-13). Over the 400 years of existence since the days of Joshua, the people of Israel thought more of their tribal identity rather than national identity, as seen in the book of Judges. David was successful in unifying the northern and southern tribes by centralizing the government in Jerusalem. Jerusalem was a wise choice politically and served to create harmony and unity between the two factions. David expanded his kingdom on all sides. Through his many victories, David gained control of nearly all the territory that God had promised to Israel coming out of Egypt. Then, he rested from war (2 Samuel 7:1). David desired to build a temple for God in Jerusalem. God denied his request but promised that his son Solomon would build it instead. So David made elaborate preparations for Solomon to build the Temple (1 Chronicles 22). Through David, Jerusalem became the center of the worship of God for the Israelites.

> **Focus on the Meaning:** The Chronicler made the Temple one of his central subjects, mentioning it 188 times. David's care for the ark (a symbol of God's grace) and his desire to build the Temple (a symbol of worship, which responds to God's grace) reveal his deepest passion in life. His master passion was that Israel should never forget the God who had chosen her for special blessing in the world. (*Dr. Constable's Notes on 1 Chronicles 2019 Edition*, pp. 8-9)

Read 1 Chronicles 22:1-19. Ask the Lord Jesus to speak to you through His Word. Tell Him that you are listening.

> **Historical Insight:** Solomon was about 20-21 years old when he became king of Israel. He and David co-ruled for a short time before David's death.

1. In Mark 14:8-9. Jesus said that Mary "did what she could" for Him. This was true for David as well. What were David's preparations for building the Temple (vv. 2-5)?

2. Focus on vv. 6-16. According to these verses, what did David make sure that Solomon knew?

   - Vv. 6-10—

   - Vv. 11-13—

   - Vv. 14-16—

3. What was David's commission to the leaders of Israel (vv. 17-19)?

   Scriptural Insight: David was content to gather materials and to make plans because he saw the Temple as a way of helping Israel to recognize God and express that recognition publicly. As king, David ruled under the authority of God. As warrior, he executed the will of God. As poet, he constantly extolled the reign of God. He glorified God in every aspect of his life. That example is still a timeless one for us today. (*Dr. Constable's Notes on 1 Chronicles 2019 Edition,* p. 10)

4. ***Reboot, renew, rejoice:*** In 1 Chronicles 22:12, David asks the Lord to give his son "discretion and understanding" as Israel's leader so that he may stay obedient to the Lord. (The law represented the Lord.) Discretion and understanding sound a lot like discernment. Read Philippians 1:9-10. We can ask the Lord for help in discerning what is best so that we can receive guidance and stay obedient to the Lord as well. In what area(s) of your life do you need discretion and understanding from the Lord so you can receive guidance or choose obedience in that area?

Respond to the Lord about what He's shown you today.

DAY TWO STUDY

Ask the Lord Jesus to speak to you through His Word. Tell Him that you are listening.

I like to organize stuff and sometimes people. But when I read this section of 1 Chronicles (chapters 23-27), I was blown away by King David's skill at organizing the kingdom for future success. David was an organizer. A very gifted man. Poet, musician, statesman, leader, delegator, administrator. And he was a man after God's own heart, yet hardly a perfect man. He messed up in some big ways yet bounced back to success. Wow!

We are just going to scan these 5 chapters to get a better feel for David's organizational skills used to serve God. If you are an organizer, you are going to love this section! Besides setting aside massive material resources for building the Temple, David also arranged for its administration, security, and worship teams. David included large groups of people for ministry teams to lead Israel in every area—especially worshiping God. David gathered together all the leaders of Israel, as well as the priests, the Levites, the gatekeepers, and the musicians (1 Chronicles 23:1-5) and gave them specific functions.

We'll look at each of these groups separately because they keep popping up in 2 Chronicles. It helps to know who the players are on the team. Remember, the Chronicler tried to include necessary information for the returning exiles to reboot their worship of God in Israel's land again. It's almost like he was saying, "Let's see what King David did. We'll copy that."

The priests

The priests of Israel were males from the tribe of Levi who fit certain physical and age qualifications in order to serve (Leviticus 21 and 22). In addition, they also had to be descended from Aaron, Moses' brother. Priests had to remain ceremonially clean to perform their duties before a holy God. Serving as mediators between the Israelites and God, they were the ones who performed animal sacrifices on behalf of the people (1 Chronicles 6:49). It was only the priests who were permitted to enter the Holy Place in the Tabernacle and, later, the Temple where they burned incense representing the prayers of the people rising up to God.

5. Read 1 Chronicles 24:1-6 and 19. How did David organize those who would serve as priests at the Tabernacle in Gibeon, the tent housing the Ark in Jerusalem, and later the Temple?

> **Scriptural Insight:** The book of Luke shows this system was still practiced 1,000 years later for the priests serving at the Temple. Abijah's descendant Zechariah served on such a priestly rotation. *"Once when Zechariah's division was on duty and he was serving as priest before God, he was chosen by lot, according to the custom of the priesthood, to go into the Temple of the Lord and burn incense (Luke 1:8-9)."* That's organization that works!

The Levites

All priests had to be from the tribe of Levi (Levites) and specifically descendants of Aaron according to the Law. Those from the tribe of Levi who did not descend from Aaron had other duties to perform and were collectively called "the Levites" to distinguish them from the priests. They were supported by their own farms as well as by tithes given to the Lord.

6. Read 1 Chronicles 23:1-6, 24-32.

    • What were the duties of the Levites?

    • How was this group divided (vv. 4-5)? See also 1 Chronicles 24:31.

    Focus on the Meaning: The Levites were supposed to serve as teachers and administrators of God's Law in their home districts (judges and officials, v. 4). During their turn to serve God at the Temple (determined by casting lots for the rotation, 1 Chronicles 24:31), they supported the worship of God's people meeting together. In that way, they were similar to pastors and church staff in today's local congregations.

The Musicians

What else is needed in congregational worship? Music, of course. Chronicles has a soundtrack—the Levitical musicians keep showing up at key points in history. The worship of God brings the people together as one community where they experience the joy of delighting in God.

7. Read 1 Chronicles 25:1-8.

    • What do you learn about the musicians in 1 Chronicles 25:1-8?

    • The term "prophesying" in the Old Testament when used in the context of worship is an enthusiastic praising of God inspired by the Holy Spirit. Read Ephesians 5:18-20 and Colossians 3:16 for New Testament examples of this same activity in Christians.

    Focus on the Meaning: David divided the gifted Levites for the worship band (singers, harps, lyres, and cymbals) into groups of 12 who would serve for 2 weeks as praise and worship leaders. That certainly shows priority for praising God publicly. Don't you love it!

The Gatekeepers

The Temple built by Solomon covered a large area of land and had many gates, storehouses, and other needs for security. Today's temple mount in Jerusalem spans 45 acres. Gatekeepers were Levites who served in specific functions for the Tabernacle and future Temple. David got the process organized (1 Chronicles 26:1-11).

8. What were the duties of the gatekeepers (1 Chronicles 26:12-18)? See also 1 Chronicles 9:22-29.

The Treasurers and Other Officials

9. What were the duties of the treasurers (1 Chronicles 26:20-28)?

10. Officials:

-   David designated 6,000 men from the Levites to be officials and judges who worked outside of Jerusalem (1 Chronicles 23:4). Skim 1 Chronicles 27:25-31. These officials were in charge of government properties throughout the land and handling local matters.

-   Now read vv. 32-34. These were David's palace officials, not Levites. What did they do?

> **Scriptural Insight:** One of the important jobs of the Levites was to act as scribes for important documents (1 Chronicles 24:6) and keeping the genealogical records. Based upon what we've seen so far in 1 Chronicles, the job of keeping the genealogical records was huge in Israel's culture. The Chronicler frequently mentions the records kept by specific people through the years.

Through all this organizing, David gave Israel a cohesiveness it did not have before this time. Organization adds stability and security. Those especially involved in the worship of God were given specific job descriptions that could be followed. David was able to be successful at this because God was with him. God was with him because David was with God. David served God and led Israel to serve her God, knowing that was the only path to success and peace.

11. ***Deeper Discoveries (optional):*** The name, Obed-Edom, appears often in 1 Chronicles chapters 13-27. Read 1 Chronicles 13:13-14; 15:15-24; 16:4-5; and 26:4-8; Write all the tidbits of information about him. He was a common man, not a king. Yet, the Spirit made sure that information about him was included in the Scriptures. What do you learn about this man?

12. ***Reboot, renew, rejoice:*** The Israelites needed a priest to represent them before God performing the sacrifices to cover their sins. Read 1 Timothy 2:5; Hebrews 10:19-23; and 1 Peter 2:9. Since the resurrection of Jesus, why do Christians no longer need a human priest to act as mediator between us and God?

Respond to the Lord about what He's shown you today.

DAY THREE STUDY

David is old. He became king at age 30 and has reigned for 40 years. In 1 Kings 1, he is described as being physically feeble, mostly bedridden. But we see in chapters 28-29 that he is mentally and spiritually sharp. As we finish out 1 Chronicles, we read how David so diligently tried to prepare for the building of the Temple and the passing on of his love for God to his son and successor (Solomon) and the people who would be surrounding him. One of the reasons David made such extensive preparations was because he had wanted to build that Temple himself. His heart wanted God's house to be *"of great magnificence and fame and splendor in the sight of all the nations (1 Chronicles 22:5)."*

Read 1 Chronicles 28:1-21. Ask the Lord Jesus to speak to you through His Word. Tell Him that you are listening.

David called everyone together—all those you just studied about in Day Two. Add to that his army commanders, mighty men, and brave warriors from 1 Chronicles 27. David knows his time to die is very near so he exerts himself one last time to stand up and basically repeat the same commission he gave in 1 Chronicles 22 but with a new twist.

13. What does David declare publicly to them (vv. 2-8)?

Think About It: Instead of reflecting on his many great accomplishments as warrior-king, David focuses on worship of his God. Rather than focusing on what he couldn't do (build the Temple), he praises God for what God had given him. What an example for us to do the same!

14. What does David say publicly to his son Solomon (vv. 9-10, 20-21)?

15. What does David give to Solomon (vv. 11-19)?

16. From whom came the Temple blueprints (vv. 12 and 19)? See also 2 Peter 1:20-21.

Scriptural Insight: This is an illustration of the God-inspired writing of Scripture. In 2 Timothy 3:16, the Scripture is described as "God-breathed." In 1 Chronicles 28:12,19, we read that God's hand is upon the writer, and His Spirit put the plans in David's mind and gave him understanding for him to write that for others to read and know.

17. *Reboot, renew, rejoice:*

- As much as David wanted Solomon to build a magnificent Temple for God, his words to Solomon were, "Put God first, everything else second." Humans love to build and create. In that we reflect our Creator God. But we need to make sure that our projects and our creations flow from our undivided worship of God. Consider your own personal creativity and accomplishments, how do you make sure that you put God first, everything else second (including your pride of achievement)? Do you own a business? How do you make sure that you put God first for yourself and your employees, then do the work?

- Review David's advice and prayer for his son in 1 Chronicles 28:9-10 and 29:19. If you have influence over a young man or woman, how will you do the same for them?

Respond to the Lord about what He's shown you today.

DAY FOUR STUDY

David had a heart of gratitude for God. David praised God in the field with his father's sheep. He praised God for delivering him from his enemies. He praised God for helping him bring the ark back to the people of Israel. He praised God for promising him a dynasty that would end in the Messiah. He praised God in good and bad. At the end of his life, he still had a heart to praise God for all the blessings he received in his lifetime. And David's positive example produced a great outpouring of worship from the people who witnessed the exchange of power.

Read 1 Chronicles 29:1-9. Ask the Lord Jesus to speak to you through His Word. Tell Him that you are listening. This is a continuation of the great assembly from chapter 28.

18. What did David as the leader give to the Lord (vv. 3-5)?

19. How did all the people present respond (vv. 6-9)?

As you read 1 Chronicles 29:10-20 below, mark anything that grabs your attention.

29 *¹⁰ David praised the LORD in the presence of the whole assembly, saying, "Praise be to you, LORD, the God of our father Israel, from everlasting to everlasting. ¹¹ Yours, LORD, is the greatness and the power and the glory and the majesty and the splendor, for everything in heaven and earth is yours. Yours, LORD, is the kingdom; you are exalted as head over all. ¹² Wealth and honor come from you; you are the ruler of all things. In your hands are strength and power to exalt and give strength to all. ¹³ Now, our God, we give you thanks, and praise your glorious name.*

¹⁴ "But who am I, and who are my people, that we should be able to give as generously as this? Everything comes from you, and we have given you only what comes from your hand. ¹⁵ We are foreigners and strangers in your sight, as were all our ancestors. Our days on earth are like a shadow, without hope. ¹⁶ LORD our God, all this abundance that we have provided for building you a temple for your Holy Name comes from your hand, and all of it belongs to you. ¹⁷ I know, my God, that you test the heart and are pleased with integrity. All these things I have given willingly and with honest intent. And now I have seen with joy how willingly your people who are here have given to you. ¹⁸ LORD, the God of our fathers Abraham, Isaac and Israel, keep these desires and thoughts in the hearts of your people forever, and keep their hearts loyal to you. ¹⁹ And give my son Solomon the wholehearted devotion to keep your commands, statutes and decrees and to do everything to build the palatial structure for which I have provided."

²⁰ Then David said to the whole assembly, "Praise the LORD your God." So they all praised the LORD, the God of their fathers; they bowed down, prostrating themselves before the LORD and the king.

20. What grabbed your attention from this prayer?

21. What were David's requests of God (vv. 18-19)?

> **Focus on the Meaning:** All of us are called to freely and joyfully choose God, but we cannot do this unless God first works new life in our hearts. What Chronicles calls us to, then, is a participation in God's work, a free giving of ourselves to his kingdom, which flows from a recognition that victory does not depend on us and our strength, but upon him. (James Duguid, "Why Study the Books of 1-2 Chronicles?" www.crossway.org)

22. Read 1 Chronicles 29:21-30. What happened the next day (vv. 21-24)? Note: Solomon acted as a co-ruler with David for a short time.

David leads his leaders to give of their own treasures to the Temple project by bringing out his offerings. The leaders all give generously. And David's beautiful prayer that follows affirms that "everything comes from you, and we have given you only what comes from your hand (verse 14)" and "belongs to you (v. 10)." If we would only see our wealth that way. David leads his people in praise and worship of God and reminds them to stay strong in their faith as he has done in his life. They are also to support their next king and carry on the legacy of faithfulness to God. It's David's commission to the next generation. Put God first, and everything else will fall into place. Well done, David.

23. *Reboot, renew, rejoice:* Consider your own spiritual heritage. Would you like to model such godly strength and character to your own family or associates? What steps do you need to take in order to echo truthfully David's attitude in verse 11, "Yours, O LORD, is the greatness and the power and the glory and the majesty and the splendor, for everything in heaven and earth is yours?" Knowing that He tests the heart and is pleased with integrity, ask the Spirit to fill you daily and guide your steps that future generations might be blessed.

Pray 1 Chronicles 29:18-19 for your sons and daughters or any young person under your influence. Also, pray that for yourself. ☺

REBOOT RENEW REJOICE

24. What is your one take-away from Lesson 3?

Our God's powerful presence helps us to reboot our lives, renew our commitment to Him, and live a life of rejoicing as a result.

Respond to the Lord about what He's shown you today.

Recommended: Listen to the podcast "Trustworthy People Put God First" after doing this lesson to reinforce what you have learned. Use the following listener guide.

Trustworthy People Put God First

A TRUSTWORTHY SERVANT WHO PUT GOD FIRST

- Obed-Edom's name just keeps popping up from 1 Chronicles chapter 13 all the way through chapter 27. One word could especially describe this man—trustworthy.

  - ✓ He was a gatekeeper for the Tabernacle. Gatekeepers guarded the four sides of the Tabernacle (later the Temple as well). They were responsible for the rooms and treasures in the house of God as well as the articles used in the priest's service.

  - ✓ He had been in charge of the South Gate and the storehouse, probably for several years. And he had proven that he could be trusted to guard the Ark in his own house. He did that faithfully for 3 months! He was trustworthy.

  - ✓ He was part of the praise team, playing his harp during the celebration parade. *1 Chronicles 15:21; 16:4-5*

- All the descendants of Obed-Edom and even their relatives—62 in all—were capable men with the strength to do the word of God. Whatever God had decreed that they were supposed to do, they did it!

COMMISSION TO THE NEXT GENERATION TO PUT GOD FIRST

- David called Solomon to his side and commissioned him with the building of the house for the Lord, the God of Israel. *1 Chronicles 22:12-13*

- David called together the leaders of Israel and commissioned them to do three things: devote their own hearts to the Lord, help his son Solomon, and build that Temple for God! David's commission to the current generation and the next generation was to put God first!

- When David knew his time to die was near, so he repeated the same commission but with a new twist. Summoning all the tribal leaders, government officials, army commanders, priestly leaders, and his palace officials together, he reconfirmed God's choosing of him to be king and God's choosing of Solomon to be his successor. He said they should put God first. *1 Chronicles 28 9-10*

- David gave Solomon the God-inspired plans for the physical Temple, the team assignments for all those who would work at the Temple, and the weight of precious metals to be used for each article that went into the Temple. That was the inspiration of the Spirit on David. That was David depending on the Lord! It was God's house to be done God's way. *1 Chronicles 28:19*

- David modeled to Israel's leaders what it looked like to give to God as he brought out his own treasures to give to the Temple building fund. After seeing their king do this, the leaders all gave generously. David believed that everything he had and everything those listening to him had comes from God. That's still true. If we could only see our wealth that way. Putting God first in that. *1 Chronicles 29:14*

- David affirmed to all of Israel's leaders (current and future) that God would "test the heart" and that He is "pleased with integrity" (1 Chronicles 29:17). Then he asks God to keep the desire to put God first in the hearts of His people with wholehearted devotion, including Solomon. David loved God so much that he cared about this.

- David led his people in praise and worship of God and reminded them to stay strong in their faith as he had done in his life, carrying on his legacy of faithfulness to God. His reminder is that if you put God first, everything else will fall into place.

- That's how to recognize someone who is trustworthy. They put God first. They choose to approach life His way. They recognize and submit to the power of His presence.

Our God's powerful presence helps us to reboot our lives, renew our commitment to Him, and live a life of rejoicing as a result. As a believer in Jesus Christ, you have the power of His presence in you. You have the ability to be trustworthy. You can choose to renew your devotion to God every day so that it is wholehearted commitment not halfhearted. The rewards are immense. Rejoice, my friend, that God is with you.

Let Jesus satisfy your heart with the power of His presence. Then, live in that power!

Solomon

4 Ready, Set, Build!

2 Chronicles 1-5 (970-930 BC)

DAY ONE STUDY

Historical Perspective

Second Chronicles carries on the account begun in 1 Chronicles. David reigned on the throne of Israel for 40 years. The spotlight in 2 Chronicles is on the kings who followed in the line of David, so it only covers the lives of the ones who ruled the southern kingdom of Judah. Much of their lives are also covered in 1 and 2 Kings.

Just before his death, David summoned all the tribal leaders, government officials, army commanders, priestly leaders, and his palace officials together. In front of this huge group of Israel's leaders of every area of life, he reconfirms God's choice of him to be king and God's choice of Solomon to be his successor. Then, David turns to Solomon and exhorts him to "acknowledge the God of your father, and serve Him with wholehearted devotion and with a willing mind, for the Lord searches every heart and understands every motive behind the thoughts ... Consider now, for the Lord has chosen you to build a temple as a sanctuary. Be strong and do the work (1 Chronicles 28:9-10)." Then, he hands Solomon the plans for the Temple that the Spirit of God had given to David, the divisions of all those who would work at the Temple, and the weight of precious metals to be used for each article that goes into the Temple. What a commission! Put God first. Everything else will fall into place, including building the Temple. Historians think that Solomon was around 20 years old when he became king.

Read 2 Chronicles 1:1-17. Ask the Lord Jesus to speak to you through His Word. Tell Him that you are listening.

1. Focus on vv. 1-12.

    •   Where did Solomon gather all Israel's leaders and elders together and why?

    •   What happened that night (v. 7)?

    •   What did Solomon know about himself and what he needed for his role? See also 1 Kings 3:7-9.

    •   What is God's answer to Solomon's request?

- Review 1 Chronicles 22:12 and 28:9-10. What had also been David's advice to Solomon?

Think About It: Solomon wisely asked for wisdom and knowledge to lead "this people of yours" (v. 10) recognizing who really was King over Israel. That was how David viewed his role as God the King's servant king. God was pleased with Solomon's heart so God gave him what he requested...and more!

2. Read 1 Kings 4:29-34. God answered Solomon's request for wisdom in several ways. What do you learn about Solomon in these verses?

Scriptural Insight: Solomon wrote three Old Testament books. The sayings in Proverbs (except for chapters 30-31) were written and/or collected by Solomon during the years he was king. Ecclesiastes was written at the end of his life when he looked back and recognized where he put value on the wrong things and needed to reboot his faith. The Song of Solomon may have been written first when he was young.

3. Read 1 Kings 4:20-21. What do you learn about Israel at this time?

4. Focus on 2 Chronicles 1:13-17.

- What actions did Solomon take?

- How could those actions benefit Israel?

5. ***Reboot, renew, rejoice:*** Any Christian can ask for wisdom today as Solomon did. Read James 1:5 and 3:13-17. What do you learn about asking for wisdom as a believer?

Respond to the Lord about what He's shown you today.

DAY TWO STUDY

Read 2 Chronicles 2. Ask the Lord Jesus to speak to you through His Word. Tell Him that you are listening.

Solomon's inheritance was more than the throne of Israel. His throne only gave him the opportunity to fulfill God's purpose for his life—to enable the people to acknowledge God's rule over them, symbolized by the Temple. Solomon does the prep work for building the Temple. He seeks the best consultants to make sure the Temple is magnificently done.

6. Focus on vv. 1-2, 17-18. What do you learn about Solomon's construction crew for building the Temple?

7. Hiram had been a long-time friend of Solomon's father, David. Read 2 Samuel 5:9-11. What do you learn about their relationship?

Historical Insight: This Phoenician king was the first to accord the newly established King David international recognition. It was vital to him that he have good relations with the king of Israel since Israel dominated the inland trade routes to Tyre, and Tyre was dependent on Israelite agriculture for much of its food. A loose relationship existed between these two realms until the Babylonian invasions [400 years later]. *(NIV Study Bible 1985 edition,* note on 2 Samuel 5:11, p. 430)

8. According to 1 Kings 5:1, Hiram initiated the contact with Solomon. Focus on Solomon's response in 2 Chronicles 2:3-10.

   • What does Solomon say about the Temple's purpose (vv. 3-4)?

   • What does Solomon say about God (vv. 5-6)?

   • Solomon asks Hiram to provide what (vv. 7-10)?

9. Focus on Hiram's response in vv. 11-16.

   • What does Hiram say about God?

   • Hiram says that he will provide what?

10. Read Exodus 35:30-36:4. What similarities do you see between this passage and what you read today in 2 Chronicles 2?

11. *Reboot, renew, rejoice:* Read Exodus 31:1-6. Skilled and artistic work like described in this passage comes from the Lord. Do you view your skills or artistic talents as a gift from the Lord? How are you using your skills and gifts from the Lord to honor Him in your work?

Respond to the Lord about what He's shown you today.

DAY THREE STUDY

Ask the Lord Jesus to speak to you through His Word. Tell Him that you are listening.

The Tabernacle and its furnishings were now about 450 years old. This magnificent portable "tent of meeting" withstood the elements of heat, cold, rain and drought to still be standing so long after it was initially created. Forty years before this time, David moved the ark to a new tent in Jerusalem for safekeeping (1 Chronicles 15:1-16:6). It was time for a reboot to replace the decaying old Tabernacle with something new, stronger, and longer-lasting.

Though in a shorter version than what is in 1 Kings, 2 Chronicles chapters 3 and 4 describe the building of this spectacular structure and its furnishings. It must have been absolutely breath-taking when completed! The experience might be like seeing some of the old cathedrals of Europe still standing today except that God never took up residence in those buildings apart from His people gathering for worship. Consider how the craftsmen got to see the inside of the Most Holy Place while it was being built. What a privilege! They saw those 15-feet tall cherubim guarding the place for the ark to rest. I hope they were awed by the cedar-lined walls adorned with gold and precious gems and the thick, embroidered curtain hanging down between the place where God would reside and the rest of the building. The Temple proper is twice the size of the Tabernacle, and the plan includes many surrounding buildings.

12. Read 2 Chronicles 3:1. Review 1 Chronicles 21:18-19, 25-30, and 22:1.

- Where was the Temple to be built?

- How did that site get designated?

> **Scriptural Insight:** This is the only Old Testament passage (2 Chronicles 3:1) where Mount Zion (the Temple location) is identified with Mount Moriah, the place where Abraham was commanded to offer Isaac (Genesis 22:2). Zion is the name David used for all of Jerusalem. Mount Moriah became known as Mount Zion. (NIV Study Bible 1985 Edition, notes on 2 Chronicles 3:1, p. 627)

13. Skim 2 Chronicles 3:2-17. What grabbed your attention?

14. Skim 2 Chronicles 4:1-11 and 19-22. What grabbed your attention?

15. ***Deeper Discoveries (optional):*** Skim Exodus 36:8-38:20. What was similar about the structure and furnishings of the Tabernacle and the Temple? Who created the plans for both?

> **Historical Insight:** It took 7 years to build the Temple. If Solomon was a young man of around 23 when he started the project, he would have been about 30 when it was finished. During those 7 years, Solomon grew up and gained experience as a leader and also had relative peace from other major challenges to Israel, especially attacks from enemies. Nothing distracted him from his building purpose. God did that for him. The future looks bright for Israel at least for now. We can imagine the beauty of that Temple and the joy it brought to the people whenever they were in the Lord's presence there. Don't you wish we had a 360° video tour of it?

16. God created the plans for both the Tabernacle and the Temple and their furnishings. Read Hebrews 8:5. What do you learn?

> **Historical Insight:** Solomon's Temple was destroyed in 586 BC. When the exiles returned from Babylon, they built a new Temple that was not nearly as elaborate as this one. The elders who remembered the splendor of Solomon's Temple cried when they saw the new one being dedicated. They wept for what they had lost (Ezra 3:11-12).

17. ***Reboot, renew, rejoice:*** As with the Tabernacle, every furnishing in the Temple was significant. Nothing was to be left out. Only the ark itself remained unchanged. Building required hard work and great use of material resources. But this work of their hands brought greater glory to God and lasted longer than the Tabernacle did. God's newest temple—the Church—began on the Day of Pentecost, built on the foundation laid by Jesus Christ's death and resurrection. Every Christian is an individual temple of God because of the Holy Spirit's presence inside and a collective member of the Church. How has the Church brought greater glory to God and lasted longer than any of the earthly temples?

Respond to the Lord about what He's shown you today.

DAY FOUR STUDY

Read 2 Chronicles 5:1-14. Ask the Lord Jesus to speak to you through His Word. Tell Him that you are listening.

It's celebration time! The building is complete (959 BC). But without God's presence, it is just a building.

18. Who came together in Jerusalem during the Feast of Tabernacles that year ("festival in the seventh month")?

19. Describe the scene in vv. 4-7, 11-12.

20. What do you learn about the ark, Israel's most prized possession (v .10)? See Hebrews 9:4 to see what is missing from it after 450 years (1440-960 BC)?

21. As the assembled people were singing praises to the Lord, what happened (vv. 13-14)?

22. This is not the first time that God revealed His presence as a cloud.

- Read Exodus 13:20-22. How did God reveal Himself to His people coming out of Egypt?

- Read Exodus 40:34-38. How did God inaugurate the Tabernacle and continue to lead the people?

23. Read Acts 2:1-4. What did God do to inaugurate His new temple (every Christian) on the day of Pentecost?

Historical Insight: According to Ezekiel 10:3-5, 18-19, God's cloud of glory departed from Solomon's Temple before it was destroyed by Nebuchadnezzar in 586. After the exile, His glory apparently returned to the new Temple built by Zerubbabel. One day, the Messiah Himself would be present there (Haggai 2:9 and Zechariah 2:10; 8:3).

As magnificent as the Temple was for Israel to see, only a few could enter it. Once the Temple was finished and God had taken residence in it, only the High Priest could go into the Most Holy Place once a year. The priests could be inside the main hall of the Temple (the Holy Place). If the doors were kept open during the day, people on the outside might get a peek inside, but they couldn't go inside. According to Hebrews 9:24, Jesus Christ entered heaven to represent us as our High Priest before God. Now, every believer can enter the presence of God at any time with confidence (Hebrews 10:19-22). What a gift!

Scriptural Insight: Chronicles teaches us about Jesus. In Jesus, God comes near to us, and the Church is united into a temple of which Jesus is the cornerstone. Jesus' perfect life and death on the cross sets us free from the curse of Adam's sin, and through repentance and faith in Christ, we are freed from the past and become a new creation. And Jesus is both the man who perfectly and freely chooses God in our place, as well as the God who gives new life to our cold hearts. In teaching us about these themes, Chronicles points us forward to the one greater than David and Solomon, to the greater temple, God's only-begotten Son come in the flesh for our salvation, Jesus Christ. (James Duguid, "Why Study the Books of 1-2 Chronicles?" www.crossway.org)

24. **Reboot, renew, rejoice:** Rejoice as you respond to God with any creative means to thank Him for the privilege of bearing His glory today and of being in His presence at any time because of your faith in Jesus Christ.

REBOOT RENEW REJOICE

25. What is your one take-away from Lesson 4?

Our God's powerful presence helps us to reboot our lives, renew our commitment to Him, and live a life of rejoicing as a result.

> **Recommended:** Listen to the podcast "Celebrating God's Presence with Us" after doing this lesson to reinforce what you have learned. Use the following listener guide.

Celebrating God's Presence with Us

BUILDING IN HIS NAME

- The Tabernacle had endured as Israel's worship center for more than 400 years. It had been moved repeatedly throughout the 40 years the people of Israel wandered in the desert. Even after being brought to the promised land, it had been moved several times.

- Solomon was crowned king at the Tabernacle and sought the Lord's guidance. That night, God appeared to him and offered Solomon anything he wanted. God was testing this 20-year-old man to see what was really in his heart.

- Solomon asked God, "Give me wisdom and knowledge to lead this people of yours." He recognized with those words that God was the real King over Israel. God was pleased with Solomon's heart desire so God gave him what he asked and more.

- To oversee the actual building of the Temple, God provided a contractor named Huram-Abi whom God had gifted with training, experience and artistic skill. He knew how to do metalwork, weaving, embroidery and engraving. He could execute any design given to him and was able to work with others.

- The building of the Temple took 7 years. During that time, the craftsmen got to see the inside of the Temple while it was being built, including all the beautiful furniture and the Most Holy Place—the place where God would take up residence with His people above the Ark. Once the Temple was finished and God had taken residence in it, only the priests could go inside.

- During those 7 years, Solomon gained experience as a king and leader. He also had relative peace from other major challenges to Israel—especially attacks from enemies. Nothing distracted him from his building purpose. God did that for him.

CELEBRATING GOD'S PRESENCE

- The building is complete. It's time to celebrate. But without God's presence, it is just a building.

- Several months after the Temple was completed, the Levites took the Ark out of the tent that housed it and brought it to the new Temple. The priests then brought the Ark to its place in the inner sanctuary of the Temple, called the Most Holy Place. They put it beneath the wings of the cherubim that extended across the width of the Ark and its carrying poles.

- While this transfer of the Ark was happening, the Levite musicians stood and played their cymbals, harps and lyres while 120 priests sounding trumpets. Joining them stood a Levite choir singing praises to God: "He is good; His love endures forever."

- At that time, the Temple of the Lord was filled with the cloud of the glory of the Lord. The priests could not perform their service of offering incense and lighting the Menorah because of the cloud, for the glory of the Lord filled the Temple of God. The cloud represented the presence of God. God inaugurated His Tabernacle and His Temple the same way—with the cloud of His glory. *Exodus 40:34-38*

- As magnificent as the Temple was for Israel to see, only a few could enter it. Once the Temple was finished and God had taken residence in it, only the High Priest could go into the Most Holy Place once a year. The priests could be inside the main hall of the Temple (the Holy Place). If the doors were kept open during the day, people on the outside might get a peek inside, but they couldn't go inside. Yet, they knew that God was present with them.

- Jesus Christ entered heaven to represent us as our High Priest before God. Now, every believer can enter the presence of God at any time with confidence. *Hebrews 9:24; 10:19-22*

- But even more than that, we have the power of our God's presence with us 24/7. After Jesus' resurrection, God sent the Holy Spirit to inaugurate His new temple—those who put their faith in His son. Because the Holy Spirit comes to live inside of us, we bear God's glory today. Everyone from young to old, laborer to accountant, lower class to royalty, church staff and non-church staff. We all have equal access to the power of God's presence by our faith in Jesus Christ.

- On the day of Pentecost when the Spirit was given (Acts 2), God inaugurated His new Temple (individual believers) with a visible fire—just like He did for the Tabernacle and the Temple. Though we don't see the flames of fire on the heads of new believers now, we can certainly see the presence of God in them when we see changed lives—men and women who are "on fire" for Jesus. *Acts 2:1-4, 33*

- Today, we don't need to go to a Temple building or pray in a certain direction toward a Temple building to see God or to experience His presence. He is inside each of us. We are each in His presence all the time because we are His temple. Whenever you are with your Christian sisters and brothers, you are in the presence of God. When anyone loves God wholeheartedly, it shows in their lives. That gives us even more reasons to rejoice than Solomon and his contemporaries had!

Let Jesus satisfy your heart with the power of His presence. Then, live in that power!

Solomon

5 The Joy of God's Presence

2 Chronicles 6-9 (970-930 BC)

DAY ONE STUDY

After Solomon established his throne over a unified nation, solidified his authority, and squashed early rebellions, he then built the magnificent Temple of God, using the plans God gave to his father, David. Building the Temple was a task reserved for Solomon since the time he was a boy. Several months after the Temple was completed, Solomon summoned all the leaders of Israel's tribes to Jerusalem. When everyone arrived, the Levites took the Ark out of the tent that housed it and brought it to the new Temple. The priests then brought the Ark to its place in the inner sanctuary of the Temple, called the Most Holy Place. They put it beneath the wings of the cherubim that extended across the width of the Ark and its carrying poles.

The priests withdrew from inside the Temple. The altar was in front of the Temple. On the east side of the altar, the Levite musicians dressed in fine linen stood and played their cymbals, harps, and lyres. Adding to the orchestra were 120 priests sounding trumpets. Then, joining them stood a Levite choir raising their voices in praise to the Lord and singing: "He is good; his love endures forever." Then, God inaugurated His new Temple with the cloud of His glory as He had done for the Tabernacle 400 years earlier. God was present with His people.

Ask the Lord Jesus to speak to you through His Word. Tell Him that you are listening.

1. Read 2 Chronicles 5:13-6:11. Of what does Solomon remind the people in 6:4-11?

Focus on the Meaning: "Name" is used frequently in chapters 6-9 referring to God. His name (Hebrew, *Yhwh*) means "I am" and signifies His self-revelation as a person.

Read 2 Chronicles 6:12-21.

2. Solomon knelt down before the assembly and spread out his hands before heaven (v. 13). What did he say about God?

3. What did he ask of God (vv. 16-21)?

Scriptural Insight: Jerusalem was God's choice as well as David's choice (vs. 6, 7). Israel entertains no pagan notion that God could dwell in a man-made house when the heavens could not contain Him. Verses 21-42 give the place and plan of the Temple in the future relationship of God and Israel. Daniel, in a foreign land, opens his window toward Jerusalem to pray (Daniel 6:10). (Dr. J. Vernon McGee, *Notes & Outlines 1 & 2 Chronicles,* p. 9)

4. Solomon then includes 7 "when we do this, please do this" kinds of requests. Skim 6:22-39 to fill out the chart below.

Verse	Situation	What he asked God to do?
vv. 22-23		
vv. 24-25		
vv. 26-27		
vv. 28-31		
vv. 32-33		
vv. 34-35		
vv. 36-39		

Historical Insight: Remember that many of the "when" situations were related to Israel in the land that belonged to God. We as believers in Jesus Christ are no longer under the same curses for disobedience that Israel was under. The Church is separate from the nation of Israel. However, what God desires for our hearts regarding faith in Him has not changed.

5. How will the Temple help Israel fulfill its purpose to reach other nations for God (vv. 32-33)?

6. What is his closing request in vv. 40-42?

After Solomon's very public act of installing the ark in its proper place, he praised God for fulfilling His promises to Israel, especially those God had made to David (Solomon to be king, the Temple to be built). Solomon is choosing to submit to God as his own ruler ("my God" in vv. 14, 40) and to God's covenant with Israel. Solomon follows this declaration with a beautiful prayer for all of Israel and all the situations in which Israelites might find themselves—both personally and nationally.

7. *Renew, reboot, rejoice:* Solomon's prayer is all about rebooting when you've been going the wrong way in life. What encouragement do you get from this prayer that a life reboot is possible?

Respond to the Lord about what He's shown you today.

DAY TWO STUDY

Ask the Lord Jesus to speak to you through His Word. Tell Him that you are listening.

8. Read 2 Chronicles 7:1-10.

- When Solomon finished praying, what did God do (vv. 1-2)?

- How did the people respond (v. 3)?

- After celebrating for 15 days, how did the people feel when they returned home (v. 10)?

God's presence came to dwell in this earthly Temple—declaring it to be His own. Very visible. Very memorable. I've always loved this passage as well as the similar event in Exodus where God comes to dwell in the Tabernacle (Exodus 40:34-38). The ark of the Covenant was present both times—representing the holiness and power of God plus His covenant with Israel. In 2 Chronicles 5:4, the ark was visible to everyone in Jerusalem that day—a huge crowd including the elders of Israel, the heads of the Israelite families, the Levites, and the inhabitants of Jerusalem, including the king. During the Exodus from Egypt, the ark had been visible to everyone present in the desert (men, women, children, foreigners, and Jews alike) whenever the camp moved. The Levites carried the ark in procession to the next location. When the cloud of God lifted up, the Tabernacle was packed up, and the camp moved following the cloud to the next location. Everyone saw that. Here, only those present in Jerusalem saw the procession moving the ark of the Covenant to its resting place in the Temple, the fire from heaven to the altar, the glory of the Lord above the Temple, and the cloud filling the Temple. Those who remained at home could only hear about it. I felt sad for them. There was no YouTube video they could watch of this event. I wish I had been there! Don't you?

9. Read 2 Chronicles 7:11-22. God appeared to Solomon at night and answered Solomon's prayer.

- What does He say in v. 12?

- Regarding the request in 6:22-39, what does He promise to the people (7:13-14)?

- Regarding the request in 6:40-41, what does God say He will do (7:15-16)?

- What is the promise to Solomon in 7:17-18?

Historical Insight: Influenced by 2 Chronicles 7:14, President Abraham Lincoln proclaimed "a national day of prayer and fasting" in March of 1863. Regarding Israel, God fulfilled that promise He made in vv. 17-18 by maintaining one of David's descendants on the throne of Judah after the kingdom split, not all of Israel. The record of the lineage of David was recorded so that when Jesus was born, He could prove definitively that He was descended from David.

- But what is His warning if Israel becomes unfaithful as a nation ("you" in v. 19 is plural)?

Think About It: The Tabernacle and both Solomon's Temple and the second one called Herod's Temple were tools in the worship of God, not the center of worship. Because of Jesus' finished work on the cross and His resurrection, such buildings representing the presence of God are no longer needed. They are still tools in the worship of God, but not "the house of God." Any building has the presence of God when Christians are in it.

10. **Reboot, renew, rejoice:** Have you become dependent upon a building or place to be the center of your worship of God? How can you worship with joy in the presence of God outside of a building or designated space?

Respond to the Lord about what He's shown you today.

Day Three Study

Read 2 Chronicles 8:7-18. Ask the Lord Jesus to speak to you through His Word. Tell Him that you are listening.

Solomon spent time and money to capture and/or fortify strategic cities and make sure that Israelites were firmly settled in them (vv. 1-6).

11. After the initial conquest of the land by Joshua and his army (the book of Joshua), some non-Jewish people groups (sometimes called Canaanites) were left in the land.

    • What decision did Solomon make regarding the descendants of these non-Jewish people groups (vv. 7-8)?

    • But what strategy did he have for the Israelites (the Jewish people)?

    • How much of David's plan for Temple worship and maintenance was still being used (vv. 14-15)?

    • What else did Solomon do that also benefited his nation (vv. 17-18)? See also 9:21.

    Focus on the Meaning: Solomon's greatness was not really his wealth and political influence. These were the results of his greatness. His real greatness lay in his humility before God and in his intercession for the people with God. He later got away from these things, but when he first began to reign, he had the essentials of greatness. (*Dr. Constable's Notes on 2 Chronicles 2019 Edition,* p. 4)

12. Read 2 Chronicles 9:1-12.

    Historical Insight: Archeological evidence suggests that Sheba is to be identified with a mercantile kingdom that flourished in southwest Arabia. It profited from the sea trade of India and east Africa by transporting luxury commodities north to Damascus and Gaza on caravan routes through the Arabian Desert. It is possible that Solomon's fleet of ships threatened Sheba's continued dominance of this trading business. (NIV Study Bible 1985 edition, note on 1 Kings 10:1, p. 491)

    • Why did the Queen of Sheba come (v. 1)?

- What did she determine about Solomon's rule (vv. 2-7)?

- What did she learn and declare about God (v. 8)?

Scriptural Insight: The witness of Israel to the world was not in going out to the nations but having them come to Jerusalem to worship. Our command, in contrast to this, is to go to the world. The Temple at Jerusalem was for all people. Through Israel's faith in God and sharing what they knew with the outsiders, the knowledge of God would spread throughout the known world.

13. ***Reboot, renew, rejoice:*** As a business and government leader, Solomon used diplomacy to enable better trade routes for Israel. He also worked hard to strengthen and benefit Israel so it would remain a prosperous nation. Your work matters to God.

- Read Colossians 3:23-24. How can your work be an act of worship?

- Your workplace (be it home, office, factory floor, school room, or road construction) is your mission field. Your work environment is where you must intentionally practice letting Jesus live His life through you—in difficult situations, with challenging people, and with integrity that honors the Lord Jesus Christ. Read Colossians 3:12-17. What do you learn from these verses to help you live out your faith in your workplace?

Respond to the Lord about what He's shown you today.

DAY FOUR STUDY

Ask the Lord Jesus to speak to you through His Word. Tell Him that you are listening.

14. Read 2 Chronicles 9:13-28. What grabbed your attention?

Peace and prosperity seemed to be firmly established in Israel. Money flowed freely. But all that glitters is not gold. Sadly, Solomon was living the life of a faker—one who claimed to know God but by his actions denied him. The writer of Chronicles leaves this out in his record. Remember the purpose of the book(s) was to remind the people returning from captivity who they were, where they belonged, and what their purpose was supposed to be as they lived out their identity.

15. Read 1 Kings 11:1-14, 23.

- Discuss Solomon's choices through the years and their effects (vv. 1-8).

- What did the Lord do in response (vv. 9-13)?

- David made some bad choices, too, as he got older and more settled in his kingship. But how was David very different from Solomon? Hint: God gives you the answer (v. 4).

> **Scriptural Insight:** Solomon's choice early in his reign to make an alliance with Egypt through marriage (1 Kings 3:1) started him down the wrong path. It is likely he married those foreign women as part of making alliances with those countries as well. David did not do this. If David did have wives who were not Jewish, he didn't let them lead him away from God. It is thought that Solomon wrote the book of Ecclesiastes at the end of his life. When you read through it, you can sense his regrets for choices he made earlier. But is there evidence of a reboot in his faith? We don't know. He would die and be with the Lord because of his initial faith. But those choices he made had far-reaching consequences that were destructive to his family and his nation.

16. Read 2 Chronicles 9:29-31 and 10:4. What do you learn? See also I Kings 4:22-28.

Scriptural Insight: Solomon's failure was worse than his oppression of the people that set the stage for the division of the kingdom. It was essentially the fact that he ceased to recognize God's rule over him and his kingdom, the very thing the Temple he had built promoted. His life became self-centered rather than God-centered. He stopped submitting to the Word of God. For Solomon, the Temple became only an outward form, not the expression of his inward life. It became an object of ritual rather than the expression of reality. In the years that followed, what had become true of Solomon became true of the whole nation. (*Dr. Constable's Notes on 2 Chronicles 2019 Edition*, p. 4)

17. ***Reboot, renew, rejoice:*** Peace and a lack of troubles are not always the best for us, as much as we long for both. What often happens to our walk with God when life is easy without worries or threats? How do you keep your faith renewed daily in the good times so that you don't take God for granted but instead are strengthened for the rough times?

REBOOT RENEW REJOICE

18. What is your one take-away from Lesson 5?

Our God's powerful presence helps us to reboot our lives, renew our commitment to Him, and live a life of rejoicing as a result.

Respond to the Lord about what He's shown you today.

Recommended: Listen to the podcast "Committing Yourself to God's Presence" after doing this lesson to reinforce what you have learned. Use the following listener guide.

Committing Yourself to God's Presence

EXPERIENCING THE JOY OF GOD'S PRESENCE

"When Solomon finished praying, fire came down from heaven and consumed the burnt offering and the sacrifices, and the glory of the Lord filled the Temple…When all the Israelites saw the fire coming down and the glory of the Lord above the Temple, they knelt on the pavement with their faces to the ground, and worshiped and gave thanks to the Lord." (2 Chronicles 7:1-3)

- God's presence came to dwell in this earthly Temple—declaring it to be His own. The Shekinah glory. Brilliant. Shiny. Very visible. Very memorable. The Ark of God represents the holiness and power of God plus His covenant with Israel.

- Everyone in Jerusalem that day saw the procession moving the Ark of God from David's tent to its resting place in the Temple. They saw the fire from heaven to the altar, the glory of the Lord above the Temple, and the cloud filling the Temple.

- Solomon praised God for fulfilling His promises to Israel, choosing to submit to God as his own ruler and to God's covenant with Israel. He then prayed for Israel and the situations in which Israelites might find themselves—both personally and nationally. He called God, "my God," asking Him to be faithful even when He disciplined His people.

CHOOSING TO EMBRACE OR FORSAKE GOD'S PRESENCE

- There is a choice. Embrace God and forsake sinful ways. Or forsake God and embrace idols instead. Embrace or forsake God. There is no in-between.

- God in His goodness repeatedly sent prophets to His people to draw them back to embrace Him when they would forsake Him and stray away. The only thing that would bring them back to their senses was total loss of what they held more dearly than loving Him—His protection, their independence, and their land. Being in a nice cushy protected environment doesn't do it. God knows that about people. When grace is shown to the wicked, they do not learn righteousness. They go on doing evil and do not regard the majesty of the Lord.

  When your judgments [God] come upon the earth, the people of the world learn righteousness. But when grace is shown to the wicked, they do not learn righteousness; even in a land of uprightness they go on doing evil and do not regard the majesty of the Lord. (Isaiah 26:9-10)

- What causes a people to forsake their God who has been so good to them?

  ✓ The influence of your peers certainly does that. 1 Corinthians 15:33 says, "Bad company corrupts good character." A lot of people who worshiped idols were still living in the land like pockets of pus.

- ✓ The influence of your leaders can do it. Solomon married many non-Jewish wives who brought their own gods into his palace and turned his heart away from being fully devoted to God. When your leader is doing this, that gives permission for you as a people to do it as well. *1 Kings 11:4*

- The only way to stay healthy is to embrace God fully and forsake anything that is not God. Forsake anything that is not His way of approaching life. That's a pre-decision—a choice made ahead of time knowing that you will be exposed to spiritual infection.

COMMITTING YOURSELF TO GOD'S PRESENCE

- Christians live by faith in an ever-faithful, always present God. Faith is a matter of loving God wholeheartedly so that you want to approach life His way in obedience. You commit yourself to doing that. Faith involves elements of hope in the unseen. Faith takes the risk of believing that God is enough to meet any need.

- Faith does not require seeing the glory cloud or the golden Ark in front of our face in order to believe that God is real. In fact, many of those who saw God's physical presence on a daily basis didn't commit to being obedient followers of God. Those Israelites in the desert who saw God's presence constantly front and center did not obey God and march into their Promised Land to conquer it when given the first opportunity to do so. They rebelled. They didn't commit themselves to the power of God's presence.

- Having an "experience seeing God" doesn't guarantee a heart of faith. Solomon saw God's glory cloud, heard directly from God in a dream and through prophets, yet still went against God's ways later in his life.

- It's a daily choice to commit yourself to the power of God's presence in your life. He is with you. You are to live dependently upon Him as though He is truly Lord of your life, not just an appendage. If you want to learn more about living dependently on Him, I recommend The God-Dependent Woman Bible Study covering 2 Corinthians.

  I have been crucified with Christ and I no longer live, but Christ lives in me. The life I now live in the body, I live by faith in the Son of God, who loved me and gave himself for me. (Galatians 2:20)

- That is commitment to the power of Jesus Christ in us. The Bible says He is here with us and in us. When we commit to living by His power and not our own, then we can truly live!

Let Jesus satisfy your heart with the power of His presence. Then, live in that power!

Rehoboam, Abijah, & Asa

6 The Choice to Embrace or Forsake God

2 Chronicles 10-16 (930-870 BC)

DAY ONE STUDY

Historical Perspective

What causes a people to forsake their God who has been so good to them? Outside influences play a big role in that. We read in 2 Chronicles 8:7-8 that the descendants of the Hittites, Amorites, Perizzites, Hivites, and Jebusites (the original Canaanites) remaining in the land were conscripted by Solomon for his building projects as slave labor.

Such cheap labor came at a cost. Those Canaanites would reproduce and continue worshiping their own gods (especially Baal & Asherah) on the high places. As 1 Corinthians 15:33 says, "Bad company corrupts good character." Even David as king had not made all those Canaanites choose to worship Yahweh or move out of the land. The country was more united under David than it had ever been. But those pockets of pus remained, especially in the 10 tribes located farthest away from Jerusalem.

The 12 tribes of Israel had each settled in their own designated section of the land, based on where God chose to place them. Consider those tribal sections to be like counties in a state today.

> To get a visual for where the tribes originally settled, how the nation divided, and where the capital cities were established, see the maps at the end of this study guide.

Bad blood existed between the northern 10 tribes and the southern two tribes (Judah and Benjamin) since the time of the Judges. The farther away the tribes settled from the central point of worship at Shiloh, Gibeon, or Jerusalem, the less the people were engaged in true worship of their covenant God. Eighty years earlier, David struggled to win over the northern tribes before they crowned him as their king. David and Solomon maintained unity through victory over enemies, resulting in peace and prosperity. But was it ever unity of heart to serve God together?

Then Solomon married wives from the Canaanites and all the other surrounding nations. Every one of them brought their own gods into his palace (1 Kings 11:1-2). As he built worship spots on the high places to sacrifice to those idols, he became a cosmopolitan ruler. Anything goes. A little bit of our God, a little bit of our neighbors' gods. Solomon had forsaken the One he had called "my God" when the power of God's presence filled the Temple. He chose to embrace other gods as his own.

When your leader is doing this, that gives permission for you as a people to do it as well. So when Solomon died after a 40-year reign as king, the kingdom divided into two nations. There was little hesitancy on the majority of the northern 10 tribes to forsake God and embrace idols instead, sacrificing to them on high places. The influence of those idol worshipers dwelling in the tribal areas that became the northern kingdom infected Israel badly.

What happens in the next few chapters of 2 Chronicles is no surprise.

Read 2 Chronicles 10:1-19. Ask the Lord Jesus to speak to you through His Word. Tell Him that you are listening.

> **Scriptural Insight:** Rehoboam was Solomon's son. Jeroboam was not related to Solomon. He had been one of Solomon's chief officials and army generals. Because of Solomon's unfaithfulness (and the unfaithfulness of the northern 10 tribes as well), God made a decision to split the kingdom into two parts. In 1 Kings 11:26-40, we learn that a prophet named Ahijah met Jeroboam and told him that God was giving Jeroboam the 10 northern tribes to be a new kingdom called Israel. Because of His covenant with David, God was leaving the two southern tribes (Judah and Benjamin) in the hands of David's descendant Rehoboam. The northern kingdom would be called Israel. The southern kingdom would be known as Judah. Solomon found out and tried to kill Jeroboam who fled to Egypt. Jeroboam was not a descendant of David.

1. When Solomon's son Rehoboam was crowned king (age 41), the northern tribes sent for Jeroboam to come and represent them before this new ruler.

   - What is the situation in vv. 3-4?

> **Scriptural Insight:** What was the heavy yoke to which they referred? Smoldering discontent with Solomon's heavy taxation to support his extravagant lifestyle and military forces flared up (1 Kings 4:7, 22-23, 27-28). Add to that the conscription of labor (2 Kings 5:13-14; 9:22-23). The result is hostility and extreme distrust and disloyalty. Conditions had progressively worsened since the early days of Solomon's rule. (*NIV Study Bible 1985 Edition,* note on 1 Kings 12:4, p. 496)

   - Discuss Rehoboam's advice-seeking in vv. 6-11.

   - What was the result (vv. 12-19)?

   - What insight is given in v. 15 about this whole situation? See also 1 Kings 11:28-40.

Think About It: Would following the elders' advice have led to a reboot of Israel from Solomon's bad leadership to a more loyal nation? We don't know how sincere the northern tribes were in their request. Did they really want to serve Rehoboam and keep Israel united? This may have been a trap in which they were looking for an excuse to break away.

God knew Rehoboam's character and what would happen here. This was no surprise to God. God knew the nation was already divided in heart. His plan provided a leader for the northern tribes before this happened—Jeroboam. Though David had tried to be the priestly king for all the tribes, leading them to worship God with their hearts, many people just refused to change their hearts and remained a rebellious people.

But God used that political situation for His good. My limited scope of understanding doesn't see how a nation divided is better than a nation united. But I see God's plan is to provide a remnant for Himself and root out the infection of the rebellious hearts.

Read 2 Chronicles 11:1-17.

2. What happened next (vv. 1-4)?

3. Focus on vv. 5-17. Like Solomon, Rehoboam fortified cities and prepared a strong defense.

    •   Read 1 Kings 12:26-33. What did Jeroboam do to prevent Israelites from going to Jerusalem to worship God?

    •   How did the faithful Israelites respond to such bad leadership (2 Chronicles 11:13-16)?

    •   How would this have "strengthened the kingdom of Judah" (2 Chronicles 11:17)?

It likely baffles you as it does me why God would have chosen a man like Jeroboam to lead the northern kingdom. In 1 Kings 11:38, God promised Jeroboam that if he walked in God's ways and did what was right in God's eyes, God would be with him and build a dynasty just like He had done for David. Jeroboam had a free will choice to embrace or forsake God. Sadly, his insecurity led him to forsake God to keep the people from returning their hearts to Jerusalem's king. He set up a substitute religion! They were already prone to this. The opportunity sharpened their focus on God-substitutes. Jeroboam might have started out responsive to God's call, but when placed in a position of power, his arrogance led him away from God. But those who wanted to stand firm with God did not put up with it.

The political situation leading to the divided kingdom, as awful as it looked, served to further God's purposes for Israel. He does that today as well. God places His people in tough situations so they must choose whether to trust Him or rebel against Him. We don't like controversy or conflict. But it is during those times that the "cream rises to the top." The remnant of faithful God-followers emerges. That kind of political and social pressure sharpens our focus.

4. ***Reboot, renew, rejoice:*** Review 2 Chronicles 11:13-17. The godly Israelites chose to set themselves apart from idolatry—a reboot. Our New Testament word "sanctify" means to set apart. At the moment of salvation, God sanctifies us in setting us apart from sin and to His purposes. As we live our lives, though, we are to separate ourselves from sinful behavior as we fulfill God's purposes in our lives. That separation can be as painful as it is beneficial.

   • When have you made the "reboot" decision to separate from sinful influences in your life so that you could approach God's way of life instead?

   • Consider some modern examples of Christians pulling away from bad spiritual leadership and practice to join together in worshiping God according to biblical truth. What is the benefit to all of the Body of Christ when this kind of reboot happens?

Respond to the Lord about what He's shown you today.

Day Two Study

Read 2 Chronicles 12:1-16. Ask the Lord Jesus to speak to you through His Word. Tell Him that you are listening.

The Bible reveals at the end of 2 Chronicles 11 that Rehoboam married a bunch of his second cousins. Early in his reign, he appointed Abijah, the son of his favorite wife, to be next in line for the throne. And 11:23 says that Rehoboam acted wisely in dispersing his sons throughout the districts of his nation to help with the governing. Perhaps he did this to keep them from seizing power from the younger Abijah as had happened with David's sons who hung around Jerusalem and tried to seize the kingdom for themselves. Rehoboam did at least one thing right!

You begin to see the effects of Solomon's many marriages to foreign women. Rehoboam's mama was an Ammonite (2 Chronicles 12:13), someone who did not worship Yahweh. One of the striking features of 2 Chronicles is the giving of the mothers' names for both good and bad kings. You will continue to see throughout the rest of our study that it matters who your mama is!

History lovers will enjoy the numerous mentions of secular historical figures in 2 Chronicles. From Shishak (here) to Tilgath-pileser (Lesson 9) and Sennacherib of Assyria (Lesson 10) to Nebuchadnezzar of Babylon (Lesson 11), non-Jewish foreign leaders played prominent roles in the life of Judah, surprisingly by the plan of God.

5. We'll look at the last activity in Rehoboam's reign recorded in 2 Chronicles. Note: The writer of Chronicles often interchanges Judah and Israel in the narrative. Unless specifically talking about the northern kingdom, the reference is to Judah.

> **Historical Insight:** Solomon had forged an alliance with Egypt by marrying the Pharaoh's daughter. Shishak was from Libya, founder of the next dynasty of kings in Egypt. The Bible mentions this invasion only as it affected Jerusalem, but Shishak's own inscription on the wall of the Temple of Amun at Karnak indicates that his armies also swept as far north as the plain of Jezreel and Megiddo. (*NIV Study Bible 1985 Edition,* note on 2 Chronicles 2:2, p. 637)

- Why did Shishak, the king of Egypt, attack (vv. 1-2, 6)?

> **Focus on the Meaning:** God said to the people, "You have abandoned me (v. 5)." Abandoned is such an emotive word, meaning to be deserted and cast off. That hurts. God's not acting like a policeman dutifully writing a ticket. He's expressing the deep relational reality of what they have done—abandoned Him, their God! None of the other nations did that! Yet, we also see how purposeful God is in wanting them to repent.

- How did the leaders respond to the news that God was abandoning them to Shishak (v. 6)?

- What was God's response to them and why (vv. 7-8, 12)?

- What did the Israelites lose (vv. 9-11)?

Focus on the Meaning: The division of the kingdom resulted because Rehoboam did not acknowledge God's sovereignty over the nation in reality, even though he did so formally. Rehoboam continued the true form of worship in Judah, whereas Jeroboam substituted a new form of worship in Israel. In both cases, the worship became only a matter of formal observance, not a matter of reality. (*Dr. Constable's Notes on 2 Chronicles 2019 Edition*, p. 5)

Read 2 Chronicles 13:1-14:1.

6. The new king, Rehoboam's son Abijah, stood on a mountain along the border between Judah and Israel.

   - What excuses did he make for his father's actions (vv. 6-7)?

   - What did Abijah boldly declare to Jeroboam and those with him (vv. 8-12).

Scriptural Insight: Rehoboam was 41 years old when he became king. He was born shortly before Solomon became king and had many years of watching and somewhat participating in the running of a government engine. He knew what he was doing. Abijah made it sound like the splitting of the kingdom wasn't his dad's fault or even God's idea.

7. When Abijah and his troops recognized the ambush planned for them, what happened (vv. 13-20)?

8. *Reboot, renew, rejoice:* Think about your view of God.

   - Do you envision Him as being angry and waiting for you to mess up? Do you think of Him as being aloof and unaffected by you? Or is He like we see Him here as deeply loving and redemptive in His purposes towards you?

- Read Ephesians 2:1-10. What do you learn that helps you answer the previous questions?

Respond to the Lord about what He's shown you today.

DAY THREE STUDY

Read 2 Chronicles 14:1-15. Ask the Lord Jesus to speak to you through His Word. Tell Him that you are listening.

9. Abijah ruled for three years. Asa became king about 20 years after Solomon died. What do you learn about Asa in his first 10 years of being king (vv. 1-8)?

10. When the Cushite army attacked,

- What did Asa do (v. 11)?

- How did God answer?

Read 2 Chronicles 15:1-19.

11. Focus on vv. 1-8.

- What encouragement does God give to Asa through the prophet Azariah (vv. 1-7)?

- How did Asa respond to the Word of the Lord (v. 8)?

12. Focus on vv. 9-19.

- Who assembled at Jerusalem (v. 9)?

- What did they covenant to do (vv. 12-14)?

Focus on the Meaning: What the Israelites covenanted to do about unbelievers was consistent with the Mosaic Law. Yet, every human has always had the choice of seeking God by faith resulting in eternal life or rejecting Him and choosing the sentence of death instead. Since Christ came, people still have the same choice.

- What was God's response (vv. 15, 19)?

- What additional "clean up" did Asa do (vv. 16-18)?

13. **Reboot, renew, rejoice:** God told Asa that when anyone would seek Him, they would find Him.

- Read Acts 17:26-27. The word picture in the Greek of verse 27 "reach out for him" is that of a blind person groping along the walls to find the door. What does Paul declare about God's response to anyone who is seeking Him? Have you been like that in your life? How did you seek Him and know when you have found Him?

- Read Hebrews 4:14-16. As a believer, you can seek Him through prayer 24/ 7. What confidence do you have when you do so?

Respond to the Lord about what He's shown you today.

DAY FOUR STUDY

Read 2 Chronicles 16:1-16:14. Ask the Lord Jesus to speak to you through His Word. Tell Him that you are listening.

14. After 20 more years of peace, Asa was once again threatened with war.

- In the face of danger, what did Asa choose to do (vv. 1-6)?

Focus on the Meaning: Hiring foreign troops brought Asa into a foreign alliance, which showed lack of trust in the Lord. Other examples of condemned foreign alliances are found in the reigns of Asa's descendants—Jehoshaphat, Ahaziah, and Ahaz. (*NIV Study Bible 1985 Edition,* note on 2 Chronicles 16:2-9, p. 641)

- What was God's response (vv. 7-9)?

- Write v. 9 in the space below.

- What is God's promise to you as a believer based on the first half of that verse?

Focus on the Meaning: The word translated "strengthen" means to make strong and courageous, firm and unbending; to support and hold up. Consider the ways that God strengthens you.

15. How did Asa respond to God and His messenger (v. 10)?

16. How destructive was his anger against God (v. 12)?

When his land was threatened by the King of Israel, Asa may have thought he had enough experience to work out a plan on his own. He took something acceptable from his culture to get results. It worked. But at what cost to his people (who were now beholden to the king of Aram) and to his own soul?

I can hear the excuses being made in Asa's mind. "I had a brilliant idea, and it worked. I saved your people, God." God said to him, "I didn't need you to save them. That's my job. I'll do it my way." Foreign alliances were the world's way of dealing with your enemies, not God's way for Judah to do it. The king and the people were to trust in God, who had never failed them yet!

Is this a typical human pattern? Do we become more vulnerable to relying on our own experience more than on God as we grow older? How often do we think we can work out our plans on our own?

God reminds Asa and us that there are no favorites with God. If your heart is fully His, He will strengthen you in whatever job you are doing—engineer, servant, mom, dad, teacher, landscaper, or IT professional. Leave no room for excuses. Stay fully committed to Him.

17. ***Reboot, renew, rejoice:***

- Have you used an acceptable cultural practice to gain your desired results only to realize that it came with unintended baggage?

- How will you choose to trust God with your need next time and ask for Him to provide the solution?

REBOOT RENEW REJOICE

18. What is your one take-away from Lesson 6?

Our God's powerful presence helps us to reboot our lives, renew our commitment to Him, and live a life of rejoicing as a result.

Respond to the Lord about what He's shown you today.

> **Recommended:** Listen to the podcast "Taking the Dangerous Road of Making Excuses" after doing this lesson to reinforce what you have learned. Use the following listener guide.

Taking the Dangerous Road of Making Excuses

To make an excuse is to release oneself from an obligation or duty or to remove the blame off oneself by placing it on something or someone else.

EXCUSES SPLIT THE KINGDOM

- The people of Israel asked their new king Rehoboam, Solomon's 41-year-old son, to lighten the heavy load of labor and taxation on them. Rehoboam consulted the Jewish elders who advised him to be kind to the people and give them a favorable answer.

- Rehoboam rejected that answer. So he consulted his peers who had grown up with him and were serving him now. They told Rehoboam to be harsher than Solomon was.

- Rehoboam answered harshly to the northern tribes. They left for home and made a man named Jeroboam their king. The kingdom was split into Israel and Judah.

- The next king Abijah made excuses for Rehoboam's bad behavior, trying to make it sound like the splitting of the kingdom wasn't his dad's fault or even God's idea.

EXCUSES SET UP GOD SUBSTITUTES

- Jeroboam had been Solomon's general. He was not an heir of David. God had hand-picked Jeroboam to lead the northern tribes. Instead of being grateful and faithful to God, he walked away from God and led a lot of other people to do the same.

- With the excuse that he didn't want the people to have to go to Jerusalem any longer for their worship, Jeroboam set up his own worship center, made God-substitutes with idols for the worship center, began sacrifices to them, and appointed his own priests. He set up a substitute religion!

- Jeroboam might have started out responsive to God's call, but when placed in a position of power, his arrogance led him away from God on the dangerous road of making excuses.

- Choosing to stand firm with God, a lot of priests and Levites from those northern tribes abandoned their ancestral homes and moved to Judah and Jerusalem. Others followed them. *2 Chronicles 11:16-17*

- God is always seeking the remnant who are faithful to Him, who leave behind their excuses and commit themselves to His presence. But making excuses for one of David's heirs led to abandoning God.

EXCUSES LED TO ABANDONING GOD

- At the beginning of Asa's reign, he was fully committed to God. His heart was aligned with God's heart for most of his life. He led the people to give up their idols. He commanded Judah to seek the Lord, obey God's laws, and be committed to God. When attacked by enemies, Asa called upon the Lord for rescue, and God gave them victory.

- After 25 years, Asa's choice to make a foreign alliance to fight an enemy reflected a decline in his dependency on God over time. Foreign alliances were the world's way of dealing with your enemies, not God's way for Judah to do it. God reminded him that He strengthens those faithful to Him and had not failed Asa yet. Asa rejected God's strengthening hand, so God removed His hand of protection. *2 Chronicles 16:9*

- When confronted with his mistake, Asa became enraged rather than humbled. He put the prophet in prison who had delivered the message and stubbornly abandoned God!

LEAVE NO ROOM FOR EXCUSES

- How do you go from being so in tune with God to being so angry! God had not changed. Asa changed. What happened?

  ✓ *Do rest and prosperity lead us to relax our trust on God and rely too much on our experiences?* God is in the human development business. Troubles both test and strengthen our faith in Him as we rely on Him for deliverance. An easy life lessens our perceived need of God so we depend less on God.

  ✓ *Is this a typical human pattern, especially for those who have a position of power and authority?* We see this in the news every day. People in authority who started out as humble servants of their constituents become dictators and become "my way or the highway" kinds of leaders. The power of His presence with you will strengthen you to be the best leader you can be, trusting Him more than trusting yourself.

  ✓ *Do we become more vulnerable to relying on our own experience rather than on God as we grow older?* Regardless of whether we are in leadership or not, all of life is ministry for the Lord—work, play, church, social, and personal. We still need to depend on His guidance. It's His choice of how to use our skills and experience.

- Have you started relying on your own experience more than on God as you've grown older? If so, stop and renew your relationship with God. Tell him that your heart is fully committed to Him and rely on His Word and His guidance more than on your peers, social media, or emotions. Don't take the dangerous road of making excuses. Stay fully committed to Him. God is with you.

Our God's powerful presence helps us to reboot our lives, renew our commitment to Him, and live a life of rejoicing as a result.

Let Jesus satisfy your heart with the power of His presence. Then, live in that power!

Jehoshaphat & Jehoram

Old Testament Disciplemaking

2 Chronicles 17-21 (870-841 BC)

DAY ONE STUDY

Historical Perspective

As Solomon inherited David's kingdom, the seeds of discontent became apparent. The Israelites chafed under heavy taxation and forced labor. Upon Solomon's death, they sought relief, which finally came but only through permanent division. The prophet Ahijah appeared to one of Solomon's officials, Jeroboam, and prophesied the divided kingdom, ordaining Jeroboam king over Israel. Solomon's son Rehoboam proved himself foolish and unworthy to rule, and the northern tribes rallied around Jeroboam. When the dust cleared, the United Kingdom was no more. Jeroboam, however, refused to obey God's Word. He founded a counterfeit religious system and led his nation on the pathway to ruin. Israel's history featured religious apostasy and unstable leadership.

After the split, the Levites from all over Israel sided with Rehoboam and flocked to Jerusalem to continue their duties. But a cycle of righteousness and corruption characterized the throne there too. Some kings were completely evil, disregarding God's Law and leading the people into sinful behaviors. A few kings started off as righteous but fell away. Others strayed but repented. Yet, several kings chose to serve the Lord rather than idols and were honored with the epitaph "he did right in the sight of the LORD." Jehoshaphat was one of those kings.

Read 2 Chronicles 17:1-19. Ask the Lord Jesus to speak to you through His Word. Tell Him that you are listening.

1. What do you learn about Jehoshaphat in vv. 1-6?

Think About It: Jehoshaphat was 35 when he became king (2 Chronicles 20:31). As a boy and a young man, Jehoshaphat's father Asa was committed to God. I think that certainly helped Jehoshaphat to get a good start. But as king, he made the choice to continue following God. He had a chance to reboot what a king should be after his father's failings.

2. Looking at vv. 7-9, discuss what Jehoshaphat intentionally did for his people.

Read 2 Chronicles 19:4-11.

3. Discuss what Jehoshaphat intentionally did with and for his people (vv. 4-7).

> **Historical Insight:** "The Lord will rule (judge)" was the meaning of Jehoshaphat's name. It was also the truth that characterized his reign as he appointed judges to act in God's place among the people. Jehoshaphat's judges not only made legal decisions, they instructed the people in God's ways. In this, Jehoshaphat followed Moses' example (Exodus 18:17-26). As in Israel's earlier history, there were both local judges and a supreme court of appeals in Jehoshaphat's day (vv. 5, 8, 11). The king himself became actively involved in judging and teaching the people. Evidently the Israelites had failed to continue the judicial policy that Moses had established, and Jehoshaphat revived it. (*Dr. Constable's Notes on 2 Chronicles 2019 Edition*, p. 43)

4. What did he intentionally do in the capital city of Jerusalem that also benefited his people (vv. 8-11)?

5. What do all these actions reveal about Jehoshaphat's heart toward God?

Becoming a disciplemaker

Jesus Christ calls you to a new life, clothes you with Himself, commissions you with a purpose, and empowers you to fulfill that purpose. It's a two-fold purpose: to follow Him as His disciple and to live for Him as a disciplemaker.

- To follow Jesus as His disciple means to make the choice to learn from Jesus through what is taught in the Bible and, in dependent obedience, apply those teachings to your life. We call that discipleship. It is how Christians get established and grow in their faith through Bible studies, sermons, small groups, and personal devotions. Discipleship tends to be inward-focused, how you are growing in the Lord. But discipleship is incomplete without disciplemaking.

- In disciplemaking, you trust in Christ and choose to follow Him as His disciple. The difference is that while you are growing in your own faith, you are also reaching new people for Christ, building them up in their faith, and helping them reach their peers. Disciplemaking is outward-focused. It is thinking to yourself, "Hey, I just learned something cool about Jesus. I can share it with someone else who needs to know this." Jesus wants His followers to become disciplemakers like that.

Disciplemaking is intentional and relational. We must start out by asking Jesus to show us how to love the non-Christians in our lives while we pray for Him to work in their hearts. Only the Holy Spirit can open the eyes of unbelievers to the truth of the gospel and convert their hearts. But Jesus has given us the job to communicate the gospel. We can do our part by praying for them and loving them. We can also be ready to share how Jesus has impacted our lives. That's called a faith story. Your story is Jesus' story in your life. Only you know it and can share it. Someone might reject the gospel facts, but it's very hard to argue with your experience of the gospel.

6. ***Reboot, renew, rejoice:*** If the Holy Spirit gave you a few minutes to share with a non-Christian about your relationship with Jesus, what would you say? You can create a brief version of your faith story using just 3 words. Here's how:

   - Choose the first word to describe your life, feelings, situation, or thoughts before trusting in Christ. Examples: *angry, independent, manipulative, miserable, hopeless, empty, addicted, me-centered, restless, striving, confused, insecure, worried, childlike.*

     Word #1 =

   - Choose the second word to describe how you came to trust in Christ. Examples: *studied, concert, Bible, friend, trouble, observation, evangelist, spouse, loved one, teacher, parent.*

     Word #2 =

   - Choose the third word to describe your life, feelings, situation, or thoughts since trusting in Christ. Examples: *peaceful, loving, trusting, freedom, servant, hopeful, compassionate, confident.*

     Word #3 =

Using your three words, create 1-2 sentences for each word—just a brief explanation how each word relates to your story. 3 words + 1 or 2 sentences per word = 3–6 sentences to tell your story. How simple is that! See the example below. Then, write your story in the space on top of the next page.

You could get the conversation with another woman started by asking her, "What 3 words would you use to describe your life story?" Then, share yours.

Example: "Before coming to faith in Jesus Christ, I was **ME-CENTERED** and thought I was in control of my life. If I wanted something to happen (specifically, get a boyfriend!), I had to make it happen! My sisters came to faith before I did, and through them I saw a lack in my own life. When I heard an **EVANGELIST** on TV present the gospel, I realized what the lack was. It was a Person, Jesus Christ, and I prayed and asked Him to forgive my sins. Now, I am most blessed in relinquishing control to Him, **TRUSTING** Him with all my heart, leaning not on my own understanding, acknowledging Him in all my ways and allowing Him to straighten my paths. (Adapted from "Create Your Own 3-Word Testimony!" evantell.org)

"Create Your Own 3-Word Faith Story"

DAY TWO STUDY

Read 2 Chronicles 18:1-19:4. Ask the Lord Jesus to speak to you through His Word. Tell Him that you are listening.

After a great beginning, Jehoshaphat took an acceptable practice from his culture (making a political alliance) and used it to keep the peace, something that was God's job to do (2 Chronicles 20:30). It was common to make an alliance even with an enemy through marriage between the two ruling families. So Jehoshaphat arranged a marriage between his son Jehoram and Athaliah—the daughter of Ahab, the king of the northern kingdom (2 Chronicles 18:1; 21:6). This would produce devastating results for his son and bring destruction to his grandchildren.

> **Historical Insight:** Ahab became king of Israel in 874 BC, ~66 years after the death of Solomon. Those six decades were characterized by murder, deception, and hatred proceeding from the very throne of Israel. Then, the throne was turned over to Ahab who married Jezebel. Jezebel was the dominant member of the marriage who controlled Ahab's reign, and she initiated Baal worship in Israel. Her hometown (Sidon in the land of Phoenicia) was the birthplace of this idolatry. It had not found its way into Israel until this marriage. In God's eyes, both Ahab and Jezebel were very wicked.

7. Ahab urged Jehoshaphat to go to war against Ramoth Gilead, east of the Jordan River. Previously, the King of Syria promised to return certain cities to Israel in exchange for leniency after defeat in battle. Apparently, this was a city the Syrians (aka Arameans) never returned to Israel, and Ahab wanted it back. Jehoshaphat insists on inquiring of the Lord first (v. 4). [Note: we don't see a record of him doing this about the marriage alliance!]

   • What is God's answer to the inquiry (vv. 12-22)?

   • By trusting Ahab, Jehoshaphat finds himself in what situation (vv. 28-34)?

- God sent a message to Jehoshaphat after he arrived back home. What was it (19:1-3)?

8. The wicked have a strong pull and can make you think their ideas are beneficial after all. Such was the case with Ahab's son. Read 2 Chronicles 20:35-37. What was the plan, and what happened?

9. ***Reboot, renew, rejoice:*** Reread 2 Chronicles 19:2. Then, read 2 Corinthians 6:14-7:1. God's message hasn't changed.

    - In what situations / relationships do you think this teaching against being "yoked together with unbelievers" especially applies?

    - What is the difference between being "yoked together" and being a "bridge-builder" as an ambassador for the Lord?

    - How could being yoked together with unbelievers be detrimental to you as a believer?

    Scriptural Insight: Paul was not saying that Christians should break off all association with unbelievers (cf. 1 Corinthians 5:9-10; 10:27). He had previously encouraged the saved partner in a mixed marriage to maintain the marriage relationship as long as possible (1 Corinthians 7:12-16). He had also urged his fellow Christians, as ambassadors of Christ, to evangelize the lost (2 Corinthians 5:20). Rather, here Paul was commanding that Christians form no binding interpersonal relationships with non-Christians *that resulted in their spiritual defilement.* ... Such alliances can prevent the Christian from living a consistently obedient Christian life. (*Dr. Constable's Notes on 2 Corinthians 2017 Edition,* p. 74)

10. ***Reboot, renew, rejoice:*** Paul goes on to say in 2 Corinthians 7:1 that, as a believer, you should purify yourself from everything that contaminates body and spirit. That means to separate yourself from ungodly, immoral, and testimony-ruining activities or causes. This is especially true in our social media-driven, instant news, world. Popular causes may not

always be the best for us. As Bible teacher Chuck Swindoll said, *"Few things are more demoralizing than realizing you've been helping the wrong side. And that demoralization is intensified when you didn't even know it."* [See the "Compromise" section in the podcast listener guide.]

- How do you recognize when you are being contaminated in body and spirit by a relationship, activity, or cause that you support?

- What should you do to keep from being contaminated by that relationship, activity, or cause?

Scriptural Insight: What if you are married to an unbeliever? See 1 Peter 3 and 1 Corinthians 7. What if you work for an unbeliever or are in business with an unbeliever? See Colossians 3. What if your adult children are unbelievers? See Luke 15. Be careful about causes that you support. See Acts 13:50 and Galatians 6:10.

Respond to the Lord about what He's shown you today.

DAY THREE STUDY

Today, we'll cover 2 Chronicles 20:1-21:1. Ask the Lord Jesus to speak to you through His Word. Tell Him that you are listening.

Historical Insight:

This passage talks about women and children joining the men in prayer (v. 13). Though these Old Testament women lived hundreds of years ago, they were just like we are, with many of the same experiences and challenges that we have. They cooked meals, did laundry, and raised children. They had responsibilities inside and outside of their homes, including home businesses. They experienced hormone fluctuations and menopause. They laughed with their friends, differed with their mates, and cried when a loved one died. They wrote songs and played musical instruments. I am sure they all found ways to use their 20,000 words per day. ☺

At one time, they were in their 20s, then 40s, then 60s, and more. They wore beads, earrings, and ankle bracelets. Their hair needed to be combed and fixed, and it turned grey as they aged. No doubt, some of them, if not all, had something on their bodies that sagged!

These women also experienced fear at various times in their lives just like we do. They faced invading enemies, sick family members, and empty pantries. They faced creditors and surprise houseguests. They even had "bad" days when things didn't go right, sometimes due to their own choices. Wouldn't you love to hear their stories of how they learned to trust God more as He answered their prayers?

11. Read 2 Chronicles 20:1-19 below and mark anything that grabs your attention. Then, answer the questions that follow.

20 *After this, the Moabites and Ammonites with some of the Meunites came to wage war against Jehoshaphat. ² Some people came and told Jehoshaphat, "A vast army is coming against you from Edom, from the other side of the Dead Sea. It is already in Hazezon Tamar" (that is, En Gedi). ³ Alarmed, Jehoshaphat resolved to inquire of the Lord, and he proclaimed a fast for all Judah. ⁴ The people of Judah came together to seek help from the Lord; indeed, they came from every town in Judah to seek him.*

⁵ Then Jehoshaphat stood up in the assembly of Judah and Jerusalem at the temple of the Lord in the front of the new courtyard ⁶ and said: "Lord, the God of our ancestors, are you not the God who is in heaven? You rule over all the kingdoms of the nations. Power and might are in your hand, and no one can withstand you. ⁷ Our God, did you not drive out the inhabitants of this land before your people Israel and give it forever to the descendants of Abraham your friend? ⁸ They have lived in it and have built in it a sanctuary for your Name, saying, ⁹ 'If calamity comes upon us, whether the sword of judgment, or plague or famine, we will stand in your presence before this temple that bears your Name and will cry out to you in our distress, and you will hear us and save us.' ¹⁰ "But now here are men from Ammon, Moab and Mount Seir, whose territory you would not allow Israel to invade when they came from Egypt; so they turned away from them and did not destroy them. ¹¹ See how they are repaying us by coming to drive us out of the possession you gave us as an inheritance. ¹² Our God, will you not judge them? For we have no power to face this vast army that is attacking us. We do not know what to do, but our eyes are on you."

¹³ All the men of Judah, with their wives and children and little ones, stood there before the Lord.

¹⁴ Then the Spirit of the Lord came on Jahaziel son of Zechariah, the son of Benaiah, the son of Jeiel, the son of Mattaniah, a Levite and descendant of Asaph, as he stood in the assembly. ¹⁵ He said: "Listen, King Jehoshaphat and all who live in Judah and Jerusalem! This is what the Lord says to you: 'Do not be afraid or discouraged because of this vast army. For the battle is not yours, but God's. ¹⁶ Tomorrow march down against them. They will be climbing up by the Pass of Ziz, and you will find them at the end of the gorge in the Desert of Jeruel. ¹⁷ You will not have to fight this battle. Take up your positions; stand firm and see the deliverance the Lord will give you, Judah and Jerusalem. Do not be afraid; do not be discouraged. Go out to face them tomorrow, and the Lord will be with you.'"

¹⁸ Jehoshaphat bowed down with his face to the ground, and all the people of Judah and Jerusalem fell down in worship before the Lord. ¹⁹ Then some Levites from the Kohathites and Korahites stood up and praised the Lord, the God of Israel, with a very loud voice.

- What happened when the news of imminent attack was spread (vv. 3-4)?

- What did Jehoshaphat as leader declare about God in the hearing of the people (vv. 5-11)?

- What did he ask of God (v. 12)?

- How did God respond to this prayer (vv. 15-17)?

> **Focus on the Meaning:** Jahaziel became the mouthpiece of God for the assembly. Whether he had been a prophet before this time, we do not know. But on this occasion, God made him a prophet to speak forth the Word of God, not just to the men praying together for their nation. *"All the men of Judah, with their wives and children and little ones, stood there before the Lord."* This is the fruit of disciplemaking in all those home towns. Whole families came together to pray. The little children heard the king pray for deliverance. So when God answered, the whole family could give Him praise. Don't you love that?

Jehoshaphat bowed with his face to the ground. All the people of Judah and Jerusalem fell down in worship before the LORD. And some Levites began loudly praising God. Would you say that the people were happy with God's answer?

12. Read 2 Chronicles 20:20-30.

- How did Jehoshaphat lead the people (vv. 20-21)?

- What did God do for them (vv. 22-26)?

- Then, what did Jehoshaphat do that benefited his people and others (vv. 26-29)?

13. Read 2 Chronicles 20:31-33. How is Jehoshaphat remembered?

Jehoshaphat wasn't perfect as a king. Just like us, he made a few poor decisions. But his heart remained committed to God throughout his life—like GGGGrandfather David's had done. He responded with humility when chastised. "He did what was right in the eyes of the Lord (verse 32)." He chose to be the right kind of a leader for his people during a crisis.

The Walk from Fear to Faith

Fear is a normal human emotion designed by God to alert us to danger so we will take action against. It. Jehoshaphat took action against the danger—calling the people together and seeking the Lord's answer.

When we look at life just with our own eyes, we become fearful, pessimistic, & negative. We think to ourselves, "Nothing's going to work. I don't know if I can get through this." But when we look at the Bible and begin to see how God has empowered everyday people like you and I, the Holy Spirit takes the Word of God to strengthen us and give us courage that we didn't know we had. God has given us several Old Testament examples, including Jehoshaphat, to show us how to trust Him to walk from fear to faith. They were like we are, with many of the same experiences and challenges that we have. Our God is as faithful now in our everyday circumstances of life as He was years ago to them. We can feel confidence in His presence and active involvement, even when we can't see it. And knowing this, we can trust in Him whenever we are afraid.

14. *Reboot, renew, rejoice:* You can embrace these four consistent truths and apply them to your life for any challenge or fearful situation you face.

> #1 God loves you.
> #2 God knows what is going on in your life.
> #3 God can do something about it.
> #4 You can trust His goodness in whatever He chooses to do!

What is causing you fear today? What are your choices for acting on that fear? Apply the 4 truths to your situation. Watch what God does!

Respond to the Lord about what He's shown you today.

DAY FOUR STUDY

Read 2 Chronicles 21:1-20. Ask the Lord Jesus to speak to you through His Word. Tell Him that you are listening.

15. Focus on vv. 4-11. The firstborn son of Jehoshaphat became king. Review Day One introduction to remember who his wife and in-laws were.

- What do you learn about Jehoram (vv. 4-6, 11)?

- What do you learn about God (v. 7)?

16. Focus on vv. 12-20.

> **Scriptural Insight:** The mention of Elijah in 2 Chronicles 21:12 is abrupt. His name combines 2 names for God: *El* (from Elohim which is translated God) plus *jah* (from Yahweh which is the personal name God told the Hebrews to call Him). So his name means *My God is Yahweh*. Elijah's style was bold with no frills. His clothes were a rough, hairy garment probably woven from goat's hair and a large leather belt (2 Kings 1:8). God used Elijah to confront Ahab and the Israelites about their worship of Baal and delivered a convincing blow on Mt. Carmel (1 Kings 18). God now sends a very confrontational message to Ahab's son-in-law through a letter from Elijah. This is the only writing from Elijah that is preserved.

- What did Elijah say in his letter?

- How did God fulfill His promise (vv. 16-19)?

17. One of the saddest verses in the Bible is v. 20. After having such a godly king in Jehoshaphat, how did the people feel about Jehoram (who reigned only 8 years as king)?

Jehoram was a bad dude. He killed all his brothers along with some other princes of Judah (likely David's descendants) to get rid of the rivals and any other claimant to the throne of David. Why was he so wicked when his father had been so good? One clue is in verse 6, "He married a daughter of Ahab." Mother-in-law Jezebel and wife Athaliah were both strong Baal worshippers and women who manipulated their husbands and children for Satan's purposes rather than for God's purposes. It matters who your wife is! It matters who your mama is as well as the mama of your children!

Athaliah's influence over Jehoram was bad. He had co-ruled with his father Jehoshaphat for 5 years. But as soon as that godly influence was gone, Jehoram made quick work of evil. In just a few short years (<6), he rebuilt the high places for idol worship and led the people of Jerusalem astray. The prophet Elijah, by this time an old man, spoke God's words to Jehoram basically saying, "You made a bad choice with your life and destroyed men better than you. The consequences of your sin will be severe." He was hated by his people. He wasn't even buried with the other kings. *"He passed away, to no one's regret (verse 20)."*

18. ***Reboot, renew, rejoice:*** Most of us would say that we'd like to be missed when we are gone. Wouldn't you agree?

- Have you known someone like Jehoram who passed away to no one's regret? What was it about their life that caused this response?

- What would you like people to remember about you?

REBOOT RENEW REJOICE

19. What is your one take-away from Lesson 7?

Our God's powerful presence helps us to reboot our lives, renew our commitment to Him, and live a life of rejoicing as a result.

Respond to the Lord about what He's shown you today.

Recommended: Listen to the podcast "Recovering the Truth of Your Heritage" after doing this lesson to reinforce what you have learned. Use the following listener guide.

Recovering the Truth of Your Heritage

What we believe about our heritage influences our motivations and allegiance. No one knows this better than an enemy of either the church or America. Enemies attack by distorting history. They put their divisive slant on history by *downplaying* valuable beliefs that inspired many of our ancestors' admirable feats while endlessly *replaying* their failures or human weaknesses. Why? People who are made to feel embarrassed or ashamed of their ancestors are more easily influenced to resent—and eventually abandon—their family, country, or faith. (Randy Guliuzza, *Acts & Facts,* December 2019, p. 18)

A DISCIPLEMAKING LEADER

- Jehoshaphat made an early commitment to seek God and follow His commands rather than the practices of Israel or his father Asa who turned away from God.

- Devoted to God, Jehoshaphat organized the discipling of all his people. He sent officials, certain Levites, and priests with copies of the first 5 books of the Bible. They went from town to town, taking the Word of God to the people.

A HANDS-ON LEADER

- Jehoshaphat personally visited all the regions of his kingdom to encourage his people to follow God only. That's a foreshadowing of what Jesus Christ did. *2 Chronicles 19:4*

- Jehoshaphat publicly led his people to seek help from God when they were threatened by enemies. "We don't know what to do, but our eyes are upon you." *2 Chronicles 20:12*

- Families, including young children, heard the king pray for deliverance. When God answered, the whole family heard His Word and praised Him. God's immediate answer basically said, "Don't fight. Stand firm. Just be there. I've got it." And He sure did. Then, the king led a praise and worship service after the victory.

- God's reboot of Judah through Jehoshaphat as they recovered the truth of their heritage brought blessing and rejoicing.

A LEADER WHO MADE MISTAKES BUT DIDN'T ABANDON GOD

- Jehoshaphat did not do everything right. He gave his son in marriage to the daughter of Ahab and Jezebel—the very wicked king and queen of Israel. Then, he went to battle with the deceitful Ahab, even after hearing from God's prophet that God wanted Ahab dead.

- God was not happy with Jehoshaphat's choice to go with Ahab. A prophet challenged him with a profound question that still applies to us today. "Should you help the wicked and love those who hate the Lord?" *2 Chronicles 19:2*

- When we experience success, are we more likely to rely on our own experiences and ways of accomplishing something than to rely on God and His ways of doing anything?

- Compromise is dangerous. Here are three things I want you to know about compromise:

  ✓ Compromise with the world is usually subtle, tricky. You get fooled with what look to be good causes that serve to lure you into the den of God's enemies. Beware the causes you support.

    Scoundrels use wicked methods, they make up evil schemes to destroy the poor with lies, even when the plea of the needy is just. (Isaiah 32:7)

  ✓ Compromise with the world sucks you in through wrong relationships.

  ✓ Compromise with the world brings disastrous results.

Christians are generally trusting people. When they start running with the world, they get outsmarted really quick! We get lured by the subtlety of the world and then we get locked in by forming wrong relationships that get us entangled even deeper. It is … right to form social relationships with unbelievers for the purpose of leading them to faith in Christ. Jesus was a friend of sinners in that sense. But you must be clear on your purpose, and you must not compromise your standards as a follower of Jesus Christ. "Do not be deceived," Paul warns. "Bad company corrupts good morals" (1 Cor. 15:33). (Steven J. Cole, *Lesson 3: When Christians Compromise with the World*, Bible.org)

A LEADER WHO RESPONDED WITH HUMILITY WHEN CHASTISED

- After being chastised by God, Jehoshaphat responded with humility, accepting God's reprimand, and continued to serve God wholeheartedly. He set up a righteous justice system based upon the Law of God, continuing to recover their religious heritage. *2 Chronicles 19:5-8*

- Jehoshaphat did his best to disciple his people. He committed to follow God and represent Him well. He intentionally taught the next generation about the true heritage of those who walked with God before them. But a lot of the people just would not give up their God-substitutes. Faith is an individual response to the power of God's presence.

- Jehoshaphat wasn't perfect as a king. Just like us, he made a few poor decisions with lasting results. But his heart remained committed to God throughout his life. The Bible says, "He did what was right in the eyes of the Lord."

- God is so merciful to us when our hearts are pliable in His hands. He doesn't define us by our mistakes. Because you put your faith in Jesus Christ and choose to be His disciple, it could be said about you, "She did what was right in the eyes of the Lord."

Our God's powerful presence helps us to reboot our lives, renew our commitment to Him, and live a life of rejoicing as a result.

Let Jesus satisfy your heart with the power of His presence. Then, live in that power!

Ahaziah, Joash & Amaziah

 **Halfhearted Obedience**

2 Chronicles 22-25 (841-767 BC)

DAY ONE STUDY

Historical Perspective

During the years covered by this lesson, God sent the prophet Jonah to Nineveh (capital of Assyria) and the prophets Amos and Hosea to the northern kingdom Israel. To both nations, the message was repentance—turn away from your sinfulness and turn back to God. The Assyrians, who were Gentiles (non-Jews), repented, so God turned His anger away for a time (Jonah 3:10). God's grace extended even to the Gentiles in Old Testament times.

However, the Jews of Israel refused God's message and continued to stiff arm God rather than turn their hearts to Him and receive His grace. This is reflected in the narrative you will be reading in this lesson. Wickedness can continue through several generations unless there is a choice to reboot and stop the pattern from continuing.

In looking at your own ancestry, it helps to remember your great grandparents and then your grandparents and parents. You can recall their origin, what you know of their lives and character, and how that has influenced you. Have there been sinful behaviors continuing through several generations? In today's passage, we see how a great-grandmother still had influence long after her death because of her evil character and how she raised one particular daughter.

Read 2 Chronicles 22:1-12. Ask the Lord Jesus to speak to you through His Word. Tell Him that you are listening.

At the end of chapter 21, we read that only one son remained to keep the direct line of Davidic kings open. His name was Ahaziah.

1. What do you learn about Ahaziah in 2 Chronicles 22:1-4?

2. What were the consequences of his choices (vv. 4-9)? Note: Joram was Ahaziah's uncle.

Think About It: God protected 1 descendant (that's all He needs), the one influenced for the least amount of time by his father—Ahaziah, age 22. All Ahaziah's older brothers had been killed by raiders. Yet, poor Ahaziah was manipulated by his wicked mother as she encouraged him in doing wrong. After his father's death, Ahab's advisors became his advisers, "to his undoing." It matters who your mama is! Jezebel and her daughter were horrible influences on their husbands and their sons. Bad wife. Bad mama. Ahaziah's life was cut short. He ruled as king for only 1 year. He was executed according to God's plan. But the manipulation of wicked women didn't end there.

3. Focus on vv. 10-12.

    *   What did the Queen Mother Athaliah do (v. 10)?

    Historical Insight: Had she succeeded in destroying all of David's descendants, then the throne would have gone to her father Ahab's family line. No more Judah. **But God's purposes are never thwarted even by the most evil of people!**

    *   How did God stop that action through a godly woman, Ahaziah's sister? Note: perhaps she was from another mother since she's just called the daughter of Jehoram, not Athaliah's daughter.

    *   God often calls upon women of courage to advance His plan for humanity. Read Exodus 2:1-10. What courage did mom Jochebed and sister Miriam exhibit to thwart Pharaoh's wicked plan?

    Focus on the Meaning: Jehosheba—you probably never heard her name. She probably knew the story of how Jochebed protected her baby (Moses) from the wicked Pharaoh's decree to kill all baby boys (Exodus 2). Jehosheba likewise, with her husband, took their nephew and hid him from the wicked grandmother Athaliah. This was courage for sure. But God in His grace made sure there was at least one of David's descendants left to take the throne by preserving Ahaziah and Joash. This was based on His sovereign choice, not because they were good people. God's grace could be continually seen in the Old Testament by those who had eyes of faith to see it.

God always preserves a remnant for Himself. This boy was perhaps the only descendant of David left who could be eligible for the throne as the son of a king. Satan tried to wipe out David's line to end the promise of the Messiah. Notice that God used a good woman to defeat the evil plan of a bad woman. He often calls upon women of courage to advance His plan for humanity. God is more powerful! Praise you, Lord!

4. ***Reboot, renew, rejoice:*** Because of the influence of 2 women, very bad things happened to Israel and Judah. You probably know a woman today who is wrecking her family. Blowing it up. Maybe it is you or someone who has influenced you. Here's the good news. Beginning today, you get to make the choices to reboot your female legacy. And the power of God's presence in your life will enable you to do that when you trust in Him.

- Has there been a woman in your life who influenced you (or tried to influence you) in a bad way? How?

- What choices have you made to not allow those or other evil influences control you in how you influence the men in your life? The children in your life?

- Read Titus 2:3-5. Whether single or married, with or without children, every woman has an influence on others around her. What kind of influence are we, as women devoted to our God, to have on one another?

Think About It: Ask the Lord Jesus to help you be the godly "mama" influence, not the bad "mama" influence in others' lives.

Respond to the Lord about what He's shown you today.

Day Two Study

Read 2 Chronicles 23:1-21. Ask the Lord Jesus to speak to you through His Word. Tell Him that you are listening.

Athaliah—daughter of wicked Jezebel, wicked influential wife of Jehoram and wicked influential mother of Ahaziah—takes over the throne as queen as soon as she hears her son Ahaziah is dead. She was not David's heir. The first thing she did was to kill all her grandchildren! Oh my! This woman had no heart at all! Thankfully a godly priest and his wife (Ahaziah's sister from another mother) stole the youngest boy away and kept him hidden, preserving the Davidic dynasty. This section details the recovery (reboot) of David's royal line for Judah. Joash was now 7 years old.

5. What was the High Priest Jehoiada's plan for the recovery of the Davidic throne (vv. 1-7)?

Scriptural Insight: The priests and "Levites" all came from the tribe of Levi. But only those who descended from Aaron could serve as priests. The rest of "the Levites" took turns serving at the Temple, supporting the worship of God's people meeting together. When they were back home, they served as teachers and administrators of God's Law in their communities. In that way, they were similar to pastors and church staff in today's local congregations. They were supported by their own farms and by tithes given to the Lord.

6. How did the leaders and Levites enact the plan (vv. 8-11)? See also Deuteronomy 17:18-19.

7. What did they do about self-proclaimed queen Athaliah (vv. 12-15)?

Think About It: God allowed the people to experience Athaliah's wickedness for 6 years. That may have increased their desire for God's holiness and His way of living life instead. See 2 Chronicles 12:8. Yet, God is always working in the background of life as He was in this case. He was preparing young Joash to take the throne of David once again.

8. What did they do to renew their covenant with the Lord and reboot their worship of Him (vv. 16-21)?

Thankfully, it had not been too long since Jehoshaphat's time. About 15 years had passed. Many remembered the truth about God. So when the contaminating influence was removed, they could start again—not with something new, but with established truth. Joash was presented with a copy of "the covenant" (v. 11), which was probably a scroll of some or all of the first five books of the Bible known as the Torah. This action was required according to Deuteronomy 17:18-19.

9. ***Reboot, renew, rejoice:*** At the beginning of this lesson, I asked you to consider your own parents and grandparents and how they have influenced you. Have there been sinful behaviors continuing through several generations? Do you find yourself doing the same bad things they did because that was modeled for you? It could be sexual immorality. It could be bitterness and anger against God about something that happened or something you didn't get that you wanted. It could be constant criticism of family members.

Just like in our lesson today, the reboot can start with you. You can choose to turn away from that behavior and replace it with something good that pleases God. The Holy Spirit inside you gives you the ability to make that change—first in your heart, then in your behavior. Identify the behavior that needs to change. Find a New Testament verse that shows the better way. Ask the Spirit to change you from the inside out. Trust Him to do this. Watch what He does!

Respond to the Lord about what He's shown you today.

DAY THREE STUDY

Today, we'll cover 2 Chronicles 24:1-27. Ask the Lord Jesus to speak to you through His Word. Tell Him that you are listening.

God provided 2 godly mentors for Joash. His aunt and uncle were like parents to this boy and young man as long as they were alive.

10. Read 2 Chronicles 24:1-16.

- What do you learn in vv. 1-3?

- Joash decided to restore the Temple after its abuse by his grandmother. What one thing was especially needed (vv. 4-10)?

- When money was collected, what did Joash and Jehoiada do with it (vv. 11-14)?

- How was Jehoiada rewarded at his death (vv. 15-16)?

11. Read 2 Chronicles 24:17-27.
    - What happened after Joash's uncle and mentor died (vv. 17-19)?

    - How did God respond to that (v. 20)?

    - What happened then (vv. 21-25)?

    - How were Joash and his grandfather Jehoram similar at death? See 2 Chronicles 21:20.

12. When you look at Joash's life, you think, "How could such a turn happen?" Based on what you've learned so far, how would you answer that question?

After Jehoiada died, Joash turned from God. His DNA from wicked great-grandparents, grandmother, and father kicked in! But he wasn't alone in his fickleness in serving God. The officials of Judah came and paid homage to the king and talked him into forgetting the Temple and worshiping idols instead.

Had Joash just been conforming to Jehoiada's expectations so that on the outside he looked good? Had he never given his heart to the Lord though he had the best mentor he could have had? Had he become too dependent on another telling him how to behave and think? Was he just going through the motions with his faith in God? Somewhere along the way, there was a disconnect.

Yet, God kept sending communications to the king and to the people. They were not left without a continual Word from the Lord. *"Although the Lord sent prophets to the people to bring them back to Him...they would not listen (verse 19)."* God is constantly wooing.

13. ***Reboot, renew, rejoice:*** Watch out for just going through the motions with your faith, just imitating those around you. This can happen over time. It can also happen when we become dependent on one spiritual leader to tell us how to think and what to do. When they are gone, we are left to our empty ritualism. Your faith in the Lord must be your own, not an extension of someone else's faith. The Lord wants you to know Him personally. He loves **you** dearly. He wants you to know that. Read Jesus' words to you...

    Are you tired? Worn out? Burned out on religion? Come to me. Get away with me and you'll recover your life. I'll show you how to take a real rest. Walk with me and work with me—watch how I do it. Learn the unforced rhythms of grace. I won't lay anything heavy or ill-fitting on you. Keep company with me and you'll learn to live freely and lightly. (Matthew 11:28-30, MSG)

    If you find yourself just going through the motions with your faith, choose to renew your commitment to and dependence on the Lord.

    • Commit to reading the Bible every day. Start in the gospels and get to know Jesus well. He's the one who says to get away with Him, rest with Him, walk with Him, and work with Him.

    • Dwell on the truths of Ephesians 3:14-4:1. You are a dearly loved child of God. Thrive in that love!

    • Rejoice in His love for you and the relationship you have with Him that leads you to live a life worthy of Him.

Respond to the Lord about what He's shown you today.

DAY FOUR STUDY

Read 2 Chronicles 25:1-28. Ask the Lord Jesus to speak to you through His Word. Tell Him that you are listening.

Amaziah, Joash's son, becomes king. The reboot enacted through Jehoiada and Joash was only partial. It stopped when Jehoiada died. You could say that the damage had been done so that restoration was very hard to do.

14. What do you learn about Amaziah (vv. 1-4)?

15. Focus on vv. 5-10. Discuss Amaziah's choices and God's response.

Why would anyone want to go to battle without the power of God's presence on their side? Notice that God gave him a second chance to do the right thing. Money lost could easily be replaced by His vast riches.

16. From vv. 14-16, discuss Amaziah's choices and God's challenge to him (and to us).

17. In vv. 17-24, Amaziah foolishly challenged Israel to fight him. What resulted?

Think About It: Remember Obed-Edom? Two hundred years later his legacy of faithfulness is remembered. Does this remind you of anyone in your ancestry?

18. What happened at the end of Amaziah's life (vv. 25-28)?

Both Joash and Amaziah sort of did what was right in their younger years but not wholeheartedly. Outward conformity doesn't touch the heart. When the outward pressure or restraints are removed, the true nature of a man or woman is revealed. The goal of parenting should not be outward compliance but true obedience from the heart. The same holds true for discipling new Christians. The heart relationship with God is primary over behavior. Establish someone in a love relationship with their God, and they will want to live a life that pleases Him out of love and gratitude for what He has done for them. Otherwise, you might get halfhearted obedience. And if you look at the results, you end up with not just disobedience but stubborn disobedience.

19. **Reboot, renew, rejoice:** Amaziah made a poor decision to hire ungodly men and expect God's blessing on that (winning the battle). Did you notice that Amaziah's first response was, "What about all that money I've already spent?" God's Word to him basically said, "Don't do the wrong thing that goes against me. Whatever money you lose, I can replace that with even more." Choosing to approach life God's way is always a win-win for you as a believer.

What confidence does this give you to overturn a wrong decision you have made, especially if you have invested resources in it? Even if you lose your financial investment, do you trust God enough to make the choice to do the right thing instead?

REBOOT RENEW REJOICE

20. What is your one take-away from Lesson 8?

Our God's powerful presence helps us to reboot our lives, renew our commitment to Him, and live a life of rejoicing as a result.

Respond to the Lord about what He's shown you today.

Recommended: Listen to the podcast "The Deception of Halfhearted Obedience" after doing this lesson to reinforce what you have learned. Use the following listener guide.

The Deception of Halfhearted Obedience

JOASH, THE BOY KING

- When his grandmother Athaliah tried to kill all her grandchildren, a toddler named Joash was saved by the quick thinking of his aunt and uncle who hid him away in the Temple. God's promise to maintain David's throne is preserved. Joash was presented to the people as their king 6 years later. Athaliah was executed, and the people worshiped the Lord openly.

- Even in his late 80s, Uncle Jehoiada was a better mentor for Joash than his own father would have been. He was a great High Priest—faithful to God. Joash did what was right in the eyes of the Lord all the years of Jehoiada the priest. Joash put a lot of effort into repairing the Temple during his early years as king. As long as Jehoiada lived, Joash outwardly conformed to God's commands. But where was his heart during that time?

JOASH'S TRUE HEART REVEALED

- After his mentor died, Joash turned from God. The officials of Judah influenced a now 47-year-old King Joash to abandon the Temple of the Lord and to worship Asherah poles and idols instead. Joash was only conforming on the outside all those years, but his heart was not touched though he had the best mentor he could have had. God kept sending communications to the king and to the people. Yet, they would not listen!

- Half-heartedness is self-determined. God is constantly wooing. The Spirit of God came upon Jehoiada's son Zechariah with a message for Joash chastising him. Instead of repenting, an ungrateful King Joash ordered his cousin Zechariah to be executed! *2 Chronicles 24:20-22*

- God's judgment on Joash came swiftly. He was executed by the end of the year by his own officials who hated what he had done to Zechariah.

HALFHEARTED OBEDIENCE WAS MODELED AND ADOPTED

"He did what was right in the eyes of the Lord, but not wholeheartedly." (2 Chronicles 25:2)

- Joash's son Amaziah wasn't much better. Joash's halfhearted obedience was modeled to his son who adopted that response to God as well. Like father, like son.

- Early in his reign when Amaziah made a rash decision to hire mercenaries from Israel, a prophet came to him and said not to do it because God would not give him success in battle. So Amaziah obeyed and sent those guys back home. Good choice.

- But after winning the next battle, Amaziah brought the gods of the defeated people to his house and started worshiping them. God sent a prophet to ask, "Why worship gods that could not save their own people from your hand?" *2 Chronicles 25:14-15*

- Both Joash and Amaziah did what was right in their younger years. But it was not with wholehearted devotion to God. We see the deception of their halfhearted obedience. We see the deception of outward conformity because outward conformity doesn't change the heart.

OUTWARD CONFORMITY DOESN'T CHANGE THE HEART

- Half-heartedness is self-determined. And it is deceptive. It makes you think that you are being good when you obey sometimes, especially in behavior visible to onlookers. But when the outward pressure to obey or restraints are removed, the true nature of a man or woman is revealed.

- That's why legalism is so dangerous to Christians. Legalism is trying to earn or maintain God's acceptance by one's performance. That would include following human "religious" laws imposed by others or even self-imposed rules that you feel make you more spiritual than others or acceptable to others. But when you are forced to show outward conformity to religious laws, you're actually drifting your focus away from the Person of Jesus Christ. You will be straying from enjoying a relationship with the one who loves you dearly to practicing a religion that might make you look good.

- Here's a key truth: The heart relationship with God is primary over behavior. God wants your heart first. Only the power of God's presence will change a heart. Jesus Christ deserves your loyalty. Loyalty requires humility. Humility leads to obedience from the heart.

- How often we respond to authority by submitting to it on the outside, but inside we're saying, "I resent it." God doesn't want our outward compliance. He wants our obedience from the heart. That's true for earthly parenting as well. The goal should not be outward compliance but true obedience from the heart. That same goal holds true for discipling new Christians. Establish someone in a love relationship with their God, and they will want to live a life that pleases Him out of love and gratitude for what He has done for them. Otherwise, you might get halfhearted obedience. Sitting down on the outside, but standing up on the inside.

- God is constantly wooing us. He continually offers us Himself and the power of His presence in our lives. Today, we get that through knowing Christ Jesus. Pastor Tony Evans calls Jesus, "God's selfie." When you know Jesus, you know God. When you have Jesus in your life, you have the presence of God in your life.

Let Jesus satisfy your heart with the power of His presence. Then, live in that power!

Uzziah, Jotham, & Ahaz

9 That Boastful Pride of Life

2 Chronicles 26-28 (791-716 BC)

DAY ONE STUDY

Historical Perspective

Throughout Israel's history, God has been selecting, changing, interrupting, and moving people and nations toward His ultimate goal—Jesus coming to earth as Savior for not only Israel but all of mankind. The promised Messiah would descend from David's blood line. Satan attempted to wipe out all of David's descendants through a wicked woman who was willing to be his pawn. But God intervened and preserved one. That's all He needed to keep the line going. Nothing and no one could stop God from carrying out His plan. David's line continued for 800 more years so that Jesus could rightly be called the Son of David.

God also intervened in the daily lives of kings and commoners, continually speaking to them through His mouthpieces—the prophets. Isaiah, Amos, and Micah spoke and wrote God's Word to the people, especially those in Judah, during the time period covered by this lesson. We read the beautiful and emotionally appealing words of Isaiah and think to ourselves, "How could they not listen and worship the God who loves them so much and desires to do so much good for them if they would only listen?" But just like we do today, pride kept them from responding favorably to God's message. They had money in their pockets, food on the table, and things seemed to be going well. Why change anything?

Read 2 Chronicles 26:1-15. Ask the Lord Jesus to speak to you through His Word. Tell Him that you are listening.

Uzziah ascends the throne after co-ruling with his father Amaziah for 24 years. By the way, the book of 2 Kings calls him "Azariah." Zechariah had instructed him while he was a child.

1. What do you learn about Uzziah (vv. 1-3)?

Historical Insight: Under Uzziah and his contemporaries in the north, the borders of Israel and Judah briefly reached the extent they had attained under David and Solomon *NIV Study Bible 1985 Edition*, p. 653)

2. What do vv. 4-5 tell you about the heart and will of this young man?

3. What successes did God give to Uzziah (vv. 6-8)?

4. What else did he like to do that is similar to what Solomon did (vv. 9-10, 15)?

Uzziah was a leader of far-reaching vision, whose accomplishments included both domestic and foreign projects. He developed a strong army which used the latest military hardware to wage war with great power. We don't know what those "machines" were because we have no diagrams or stone carvings depicting them. But they allowed the army to more easily defend an enemy attack on a city and even to repel it. The land prospered under Uzziah. As a result, we read twice of his widespread fame (vv. 8, 14).

> **Focus on the Meaning:** Whenever God grants that kind of success and fame to a person, it should be used for the Lord and His purpose. Fame is simply an opportunity to tell more people of the greatness of God, so that His name is exalted. It also provides the opening to do more for the Lord's work and for His people, to see them established in His ways. George Washington Carver said that the only advantage of fame is that it gives you a platform for service. So we ought to view any measure of success God gives us as a trust to be managed for His glory and kingdom. (Steven J. Cole, *The Seduction of Success (2 Chronicles 26)*, Bible.org)

5. ***Reboot, renew, rejoice:*** When our Creator God made humans, He gave us the ability to create and to build as He did. If you are involved in construction, agriculture, science, customer service, or any other work, thank God for your skills and opportunity. You can use your skills and knowledge to glorify God and benefit others. If you own a business, you can choose to glorify God through your services and products and let your clients know that is your purpose.

   • What skill or work opportunity has God given to you? Commit that time and effort to glorifying Him and do it well. Thank Him for that ability to design, build, write, sing, serve, or whatever it is that you do.

   • What platform for service to Him has God given you in your work? How do you take advantage of that opportunity to tell more people of the greatness of God?

Respond to the Lord about what He's shown you today.

DAY TWO STUDY

Ask the Lord Jesus to speak to you through His Word. Tell Him that you are listening.

Read 2 Chronicles 26:16-23.

King Uzziah is shown as a wonderfully intelligent and innovative king, under whom the state of Judah prospered. His reign was one of the most prosperous, except for that of Jehoshaphat, since the time of Solomon. He acted properly in the early part of his reign and was considered a righteous king. But success can have a not-so-nice byproduct.

6. After around 42 years, Uzziah's success led to what (v. 16, first part)?

7. Discuss what happened in vv. 16-20.

Historical Insight: In the Old Testament, the term "leprosy" was associated with a variety of highly infectious skin diseases, including what we know as Hansen's disease today. It was recognized by scaly skin blemishes that often appeared white.

8. Why was leprosy so bad? See v. 21 and Leviticus 13:45-46.

9. What else do you learn from vv. 22-23?

10. Read Isaiah 6:1-13 and Amos 1:1. What else happened during Uzziah's years?

Historical Insight: Both the prophets Amos (Uzziah's contemporary) and Zechariah (lived 250 years later) wrote about this earthquake (~740BC). Zechariah was speaking to people who remembered how people fled before the quake. It must have been massive and unforgettable. There is archaeological evidence of 2 great quakes during Uzziah's time. According to geologist Steven A. Austin, the magnitude of this quake may have been anywhere from 7.8-8.2.

Uzziah started believing his own press clippings and his pride led to a fall. In one hour, he ruined a prosperous lifetime as a successful king. Sadly, we don't see any repentance. He just hid himself away. Maybe he stayed angry at the Lord and didn't seek healing. We saw how his GGGG grandfather Asa and his grandpa Joash had both become angry and bull-headed when reprimanded by God for a bad decision they made.

11. ***Reboot, renew, rejoice:*** Read 1 John 2:16. Write it below.

That boastful pride of life. John makes it clear that anything that produces the pride of life comes from a love of the world. It exalts us above our rightful place of God-dependence and offers us the illusion of having God-like qualities, so that we boast in arrogance, worldly wisdom, and self-dependence.

* How does that happen?

* What are the warning signs?

* What can you do to avoid it?

Respond to the Lord about what He's shown you today.

DAY THREE STUDY

Read 2 Chronicles 27:1-9. Ask the Lord Jesus to speak to you through His Word. Tell Him that you are listening.

12. Jotham was co-ruler with his father for 10 years before he was crowned king.

- How was Jotham like his father?

- How was Jotham unlike his father?

13. What information is given about the people of Judah in v. 2? This comes into play later.

Scriptural Insight: Remember that Jehoshaphat intentionally taught his people about God and His ways—first by sending priests and Levites with a copy of the Scriptures then by going himself to teach them. We haven't seen any kings after him do this. Jesus likewise went from town to town teaching the people of His days about God and His ways. Every successive generation needs to be taught truth in order to live by it.

14. Consider what you saw happen in Uzziah's life. What is (or should be) the relationship between success in life and reliance on God?

15. **Reboot, renew, rejoice:** I heard someone say that you can always learn from a bad example of what not to do. Jotham seemed to learn that. You can learn the easy way or the hard way. Read 1 Corinthians 10:1-13.

- In recounting Israel's history as we are doing through this study, what are some things we can learn not to do (vv. 6-10)?

- What is the warning in v. 12?

- What is the promise of God to you in v. 13?

- Consider that promise in the context of learning from a bad example. What does that promise of God's faithfulness during temptation mean in your life regarding those who have been or currently are bad examples for you?

Respond to the Lord about what He's shown you today.

DAY FOUR STUDY

Read 2 Chronicles 28:1-27. Ask the Lord Jesus to speak to you through His Word. Tell Him that you are listening.

As you read the first part of this passage, did you want to scream, "What?!" How could the son of someone who walked steadfastly with the Lord do such a thing? As you have probably recognized throughout Chronicles, human nature hasn't changed one bit in 3000 years. People are still as wicked in their choices and behaviors today as they were back then. God still enacts His judgment on the wicked in His time and in His way. That's something we can count on.

16. Although Ahaz served as co-ruler with his father for 3 years, what do you learn right away about Ahaz in vv. 1-5?

17. Sin brings consequences. What consequences did God bring to get Ahaz's attention (vv. 5-8)?

18. For 80 years, the prophet Isaiah spoke for God during the lives of four kings of Israel: Uzziah, Jotham, Ahaz, and Hezekiah. **Read Isaiah 7:1-17.** God recognized Ahaz's fear of attack from enemy armies and sent him a message. Discuss God's interaction with Ahaz and the sign God would give to him. [Now you know the context of this famous Christmas verse quoted also in Matthew 1:23 as being fulfilled in Jesus.] We see Ahaz's response to God's presence in 2 Chronicles 28.

19. God didn't like what the king of Israel and his army did to their Judean relatives. What was his message, and how did the Israelite army respond (2 Chronicles 28:9-15)?

20. What else is revealed about Ahaz in vv. 16-23?

21. What is his final act of rebellion against God (vv. 24-25)?

Ahaz was a terrible leader. He chose from early in his life (age 20) to hate God. Does this leave you baffled, asking why a man with a good father that loved God could choose to do such things? From Isaiah 7, we get a glimpse of the fear that might have motivated Ahaz's behavior. And when he probably became the most afraid of what the king of Assyria might do to him, Ahaz went away from God more than toward him. He cleared out the Temple and shut its doors! Not only did he reject God, he tried to close off access to God for anyone else. Someone didn't like that because he was not buried with the other good kings (v. 27).

> **From the Hebrew:** When did the Israelites, who were known as Hebrews in Egypt, get to be known as the "Jews?" The word "Jew" is the English translation of the Hebrew word, *Yehudi*, derived from the name Judah (one of Jacob's 12 sons whose descendants became

the tribes of Israel). In 2 Kings 16:6, the people of the kingdom of Judah began to be called *Yehudi*. With the destruction of the northern kingdom of Israel, the kingdom of Judah became the sole Jewish state and the term *Yehudi* was applied to all Israelites living within it—not just those who were from the tribe of Judah. In 2 Chronicles 32:18, the Hebrew language is called the language of the *Yehudi*. By the time of the book of Esther, all of the Israelites who were living as captives in the Persian Empire were known as *Yehudi* (Jews) regardless of tribal affiliation. That carried into the New Testament. In common speech, the word "Jew" is used to refer to all of the physical and spiritual descendants of Abraham, and the word "Judaism" is used to refer to their beliefs. ("Who is a Jew?" www.jewfaq.org)

22. ***Reboot, renew, rejoice:*** God tried to get Ahaz's attention to turn him back to the right way. Ahaz refused and dug his heels more and more into rebellion against God. Do you know someone like that, so against God that they try to prevent others from knowing Him? How should you pray for that person?

REBOOT RENEW REJOICE

23. What is your one take-away from Lesson 9?

Our God's powerful presence helps us to reboot our lives, renew our commitment to Him, and live a life of rejoicing as a result.

Respond to the Lord about what He's shown you today.

Recommended: Listen to the podcast "Depending on God Subdues That Boastful Pride of Life" after doing this lesson to reinforce what you have learned. Use the following listener guide.

Depending on God Subdues That Boastful Pride of Life

UZZIAH STARTED ON THE RIGHT TRACK

- During the early years of Uzziah's life, he was instructed to seek God by a godly priest named Zechariah. As long as he sought the Lord, God gave Uzziah success.

- Uzziah was a very active king, working hard to benefit his nation. He improved farming practices in his country. He supplied his army well from the national armory. And he had engineers design and build better defenses for Jerusalem's walls.

- Uzziah started believing his own press clippings. He also believed the lie that he was the author of his success. The Bible says that after Uzziah became powerful, his pride led to his downfall. In one hour, he ruined a prosperous lifetime as a successful king.

PRIDE LED TO HIS DOWNFALL

- Uzziah unlawfully went into the Holy Place of the Temple to burn incense on the altar of incense. When confronted by 80 horrified priests, Uzziah got angry. While he was raging at the priests, the Lord afflicted him with a horrible skin disease called leprosy.

- Sadly, we don't see any repentance. Having leprosy removed Uzziah from public influence. Now he couldn't even go to the Temple courts. And he was not even buried in the kings' tomb with David's other descendants. That boastful pride of life.

THE STRONG PULL OF THE PRIDE OF LIFE

- Thankfully, Uzziah's son Jotham did not follow his father's bad example. In fact, he learned from it. He grew powerful as a king because he walked steadfastly before the Lord, his God. He embraced the power of God's presence with him. *2 Chronicles 27:7*

- Jotham wasn't able to lead his people spiritually to give up their corrupt practices. The people were still using hilltops for Baal worship. It is so hard to root out bad traditions.

- Jotham's son Ahaz was very wicked! He made idols for Baal worship and worshiped them. He even sacrificed his own son to idols, something God forbid and never asked or even wanted His people to do. Ahaz was running scared. So God told Isaiah to tell Jotham to be careful, keep calm, not be afraid and to not lose heart. Then, the Lord gave Ahaz a sign, "The virgin will conceive and give birth to a son, and will call him Immanuel." (Isaiah 7:14)

- Immanuel means God with us. Ahaz had God's presence with him. He just needed to stay depending on God rather than run scared. But Ahaz intentionally rejected God's help and went from horrible to worse! The Lord lifted His hand of protection from Judah to humble the king and draw him back to God. But Ahaz let the boastful pride of life take control of his heart and direct his decisions. He did no one any good, least of all to himself!

DEPENDING ON GOD SUBDUES THE PRIDE OF LIFE

Do not love the world or anything in the world. If anyone loves the world, love for the Father is not in them. For everything in the world—the lust of the flesh, the lust of the eyes, and the pride of life—comes not from the Father but from the world. The world and its desires pass away, but whoever does the will of God lives forever. (1 John 2:15-17)

- Anything that produces the pride of life comes from a love of the world. A love of the world and the world system exalts us in our thinking above our rightful place of God-dependence. It offers us the illusion of having God-like qualities so that we boast in arrogance, worldly wisdom, and self-dependence. We fall under the deception of having control of our lives and those around us. That desire for control takes us away from God not toward Him.

- In the midst of even successful lives, God wants us to learn to rely on Him more than on ourselves. So what does this relying on God look like? We are supposed to grow and mature in our thinking and behavior. God wants us to give to Him all the skills, talents, advantages, and opportunities and use them for His glory. That involves following His leading and guidance. It means submitting our strengths and our weaknesses to Him for His purposes in our lives.

- Human parents raise their children to be less dependent on them and more independent. But God raises His children to be *less independent* and ***more dependent on Him.*** Whatever He brings into our lives that makes us more dependent upon Him is good for us. The key to being a God-dependent woman is ***dependent living***.

- Dependent living is not weakness. It is being stronger and having more influence, success, and satisfaction than we could ever have through our own efforts—as brilliant and self-sufficient as we think we are or as weak and messed up as we think we are or anywhere in-between.

- We learn how to do this as we act in obedience to the Word of God, depend on Jesus Christ for the power to do so, and trust Him with the results. This "dependent living" will make us stronger and more effective in life than we could ever be on our own because we have the power of God's presence at work in us and for us. Only depending on God will subdue that boastful pride of life.

- Our God's powerful presence helps us to reboot our lives, renew our commitment to Him, and live a life of rejoicing as a result. Why not depend on Him?

Let Jesus satisfy your heart with the power of His presence. Then, live in that power!

Hezekiah, Manasseh, & Amon

10 The Unstoppable Power of God's Forgiveness

2 Chronicles 29-33 (716-640 BC)

DAY ONE STUDY

Historical Perspective

God had promised Israel that if they obeyed Him, He would bless them as a nation. If they did not, then He would judge them and cause them to be taken into captivity (Deuteronomy 28). Both nations, Israel and Judah, were falling deep into idol-worship. Because of their great sin, God's hand of judgment first fell on the Northern Kingdom (aka Israel, Samaria, or Ephraim). During the sixth year of Hezekiah's reign, Sennacherib (the king of Assyria) conquered the northern kingdom. Over a number of years, the ten tribes from Samaria and those east of the Jordan River were taken into captivity and resettled into today's Syria, Iraq, and Iran. Assyria transported foreign captives back to Israel to join the few of the poorest Israelites left in their homeland.

It was a tense time for Judah's king as Sennacherib invaded Judah, bent on conquering Jerusalem. By the way, both 2 Chronicles and 2 Kings devote more attention to Hezekiah than to any of the other kings after Solomon. The prophets Isaiah and Micah were available to him for counsel, and they continued to teach the people to turn back to God.

Ask the Lord Jesus to speak to you through His Word. Tell Him that you are listening.

1. Read 2 Chronicles 29:1-11. After reading about what Hezekiah's dad Ahaz did in the last lesson, what is described here in these verses is a major "reboot!" Uninstall bad applications, shutdown, restart, and clear the caches.

   From the Hebrew: To consecrate (v. 5, Heb. *qadash*) means to make clean and, therefore, holy (set apart from anything unclean or sinful). For people, this involved bathing and changing into clean clothes before coming before the Lord.

   • What do you learn about Hezekiah (vv. 1-2)?

   Think About It: Hezekiah's mama was the Jewish daughter of the godly man who had instructed Uzziah in the ways of the Lord. Once again, it matters who your mama is!

   • What became Hezekiah's priority in his first year (vv. 3-10)?

   • What is his charge to the priests and the Levites (v. 11)?

Scriptural Insight: In 2 Chronicles 29:9, we see a reference to Israel (the northern kingdom) being taken captive. People in some parts of Judah were also taken captive. Note how Hezekiah still refers to them as "our" fathers, wives, sons, and daughters. His heart bleeds for the people of God who are now gone.

It took 16 days to clean out the Temple and purify it for the Lord's service again (vv. 15-19). The next morning, the king and city officials gathered at the Temple to restore their cleanness also before God through sacrifices given for all Israel (vv. 20-24), which now includes Judah and those refugees from the northern kingdom. The nation is one again.

2. Let's focus on 2 Chronicles 29:25-36. Read the verses below and mark anything that grabs your attention. Then, answer the questions that follow.

29 *25 He stationed the Levites in the temple of the Lord with cymbals, harps and lyres in the way prescribed by David and Gad the king's seer and Nathan the prophet; this was commanded by the Lord through his prophets. 26 So the Levites stood ready with David's instruments, and the priests with their trumpets.*

27 Hezekiah gave the order to sacrifice the burnt offering on the altar. As the offering began, singing to the Lord began also, accompanied by trumpets and the instruments of David king of Israel. 28 The whole assembly bowed in worship, while the musicians played and the trumpets sounded. All this continued until the sacrifice of the burnt offering was completed. 29 When the offerings were finished, the king and everyone present with him knelt down and worshiped. 30 King Hezekiah and his officials ordered the Levites to praise the Lord with the words of David and of Asaph the seer. So they sang praises with gladness and bowed down and worshiped.

31 Then Hezekiah said, "You have now dedicated yourselves to the Lord. Come and bring sacrifices and thank offerings to the temple of the Lord." So the assembly brought sacrifices and thank offerings, and all whose hearts were willing brought burnt offerings.

32 The number of burnt offerings the assembly brought was seventy bulls, a hundred rams and two hundred male lambs—all of them for burnt offerings to the Lord. 33 The animals consecrated as sacrifices amounted to six hundred bulls and three thousand sheep and goats. 34 The priests, however, were too few to skin all the burnt offerings; so their relatives the Levites helped them until the task was finished and until other priests had been consecrated, for the Levites had been more conscientious in consecrating themselves than the priests had been. 35 There were burnt offerings in abundance, together with the fat of the fellowship offerings and the drink offerings that accompanied the burnt offerings.

So the service of the temple of the Lord was reestablished. 36 Hezekiah and all the people rejoiced at what God had brought about for his people, because it was done so quickly.

- What grabbed your attention?

- What helpful information did they have (v. 25)?

- Hezekiah's words in v. 30 are referencing what book in our Bible?

- What is said about the Levites' preparation to serve (v. 34)?

- What do you learn about their rejoicing in this passage?

3. **Reboot, renew, rejoice:** A reboot requires someone to take charge and take it seriously. Fear of consequences can motivate obedience, as is the case with Hezekiah and the people of Israel. But it can also be a God-responsiveness that wants to clean up and discard that which is worthless in one's life in order to build a new life approached God's way rather than the world's way.

    - What represents God and approaching life His way in your house or life?

    - What represents approaching life the world's way in your house or life?

    - The Lord desires that you clean up and discard that which is worthless (the world's way of approaching life) and put in and establish that which represents God and His way of approaching life. You have the power of God's presence in your life. He doesn't ask you to do anything that He doesn't enable you to do. What will you intentionally discard that is not godly? Trust in Him as you reboot your direction in life to match what God wants for you.

Respond to the Lord about what He's shown you today.

DAY TWO STUDY

Read 2 Chronicles 30:1-27. Ask the Lord Jesus to speak to you through His Word. Tell Him that you are listening.

> **Focus on the Meaning:** Passover is a Jewish festival celebrating the exodus from Egypt and the Israelites' freedom from slavery to the Egyptians. The Feast of Passover, along with the Feast of Unleavened Bread, was the first of the festivals commanded by God for Israel to observe (see Exodus 12). The Passover lamb was killed and its blood was applied to doorposts and lintels of every house. God also instituted a commemorative meal for that night. Jesus is our Passover (1 Corinthians 5:7; Revelation 5:12). He was killed at Passover time, and the Last Supper was a Passover meal (Luke 22:7–8). By (spiritually) applying His blood to our lives by faith, we trust Christ to save us from death.

4. Focus on vv. 1-12. Note: Ephraim refers to the northern tribes west of the Jordan and Manasseh refers to the tribes living east of the Jordan.

   - To whom did Hezekiah send the invitation to celebrate the Passover (vv. 1-5)?

   - What was Hezekiah's message in the invitation (vv. 6-9)?

   - What were the responses to the invitation (vv. 10-12)?

> **Historical Insight:** The 10 tribes of the northern kingdom taken captive by Assyria are often referred to as the "lost tribes of Israel." The truth is they were never really lost. Many of the Jews who remained in the land after the Assyrian conquest re-united with Judah in the south (2 Chronicles 30:10; 34:6–9). Assyria was later conquered by Babylon, who went on to invade the Southern Kingdom of Israel, deporting the two remaining tribes: Judah and Benjamin. Remnants of the northern tribes would have thus been part of the Babylonian deportations. Seventy years later, when King Cyrus allowed the Israelites to return to Israel, many (from all twelve tribes) returned to Israel to rebuild their homeland. God knows where all twelve tribes are … In the end times, God will call out witnesses from each of the twelve tribes (Revelation 7:4–8). So obviously, God has been keeping track of who belongs to what tribe. In the Gospels, the prophetess Anna (Luke 2:36) was from the tribe of Asher (one of the ten supposedly lost tribes). Jesus promises the disciples that they will "sit on thrones, judging the twelve tribes of Israel" (Luke 22:30). Paul speaks of "the promise our twelve tribes are hoping to see fulfilled as they earnestly serve God day and night" (Acts 26:7)— note the present tense. James addresses his epistle "to the twelve tribes scattered among the nations" (James 1:1). In short, there is ample evidence in Scripture that all twelve tribes of Israel are still in existence and will be in the Messianic kingdom. None of them are lost. (*What happened to the lost tribes of Israel?* Gotquestions.org)

5. Focus on vv. 13-27.

    Historical Insight: The Kidron Valley runs north-south between the Mount of Olives and the eastern wall of the Temple Mount and the City of David. It was a convenient place to dump unclean things since it lay just east of the Temple area.

    - What did the people do first (v. 14)?

    - What do vv. 17-18 reveal about the people who came?

    Think About It: In today's terms, you might call these "seekers" because they show up and want to participate but don't know all the rules. Or they are like those who attended church as children, got away from the Lord as teens and young adults, then are drawn back to Him whenever they start families or experience a crisis. Point is—they are present and wanting more than what they've had in life before this time. They came!

    - Discuss Hezekiah's prayer and God's gracious response (vv. 18-20). See also v.9.

    - The Levites were what we might consider local pastors for their communities. How did Hezekiah coach his team of Levites (v. 22 and look back at 29:5)?

    - Who else joined the assembly of Jews (v. 25)? See also Isaiah 56:6-7.

    Scriptural Insight: These "foreigners" are the forerunners of the God-fearing Gentiles (non-Jews) who attended Jewish synagogues during Jesus' time. Israel's purpose was to be a light to the Gentiles. God's words in Isaiah 56:7 were repeated by Jesus in Matthew 21:13 to remind the Jews that the Temple was to be a house of prayer for all nations. You see an illustration of that here.

Read 2 Chronicles 31:1-8, 20-21.

6. Focus on vv. 1-8.

   • What happened after the 14-day festival (v. 1)?

   • Hezekiah resumed the contributions for the priests and Levites, which was their support as "clergy" so they could devote themselves to carrying out the Law of the Lord (v. 4). How did the people respond (vv. 5-8)?

7. **Deeper Discoveries (optional):** Skim 2 Chronicles 31:9-19 to see how the money was distributed and to whom.

8. Look at 2 Chronicles 31:20-21. What do you learn from these verses?

9. **Reboot, renew, rejoice:** Regardless of the consequences of rejection, regardless of what situations God used to try to get their attention and draw them back to Himself, many still preferred to do life on their own (2 Chronicles 30:10-11). However, they benefited from the presence of godly people surrounding them and God's blessing on the nation because of the response of the godly. The responses to the invitation of God's grace in the gospel message today are no different than they were to God's grace centuries ago. And those who reject the gospel today are still benefiting from the blessing of godly people surrounding them doing good deeds that benefit communities.

   • Whom do you know who responded to God with humility and faith (including yourself) when He put something in their path to draw them to Him?

   • Whom do you know who responded to God with scorn and ridicule when He put something in their path to draw them to Him?

- How are they benefiting from the blessing of godly people surrounding them?

Think About It: We humans are not naturally so gracious to those who are enemies. But God's love for us is recklessly extravagant. This is demonstrated by the life and death of Jesus Christ and the salvation He offers to us by our faith alone, even while we are His enemies (Romans 5:10; Colossians 1:21). As the song says, "Oh, the overwhelming, never-ending, reckless love of God. Oh, it chases me down, fights 'til I'm found, leaves the ninety-nine. I couldn't earn it, I don't deserve it, still You give Yourself away. Oh, the overwhelming, never-ending, reckless love of God (Cory Asbury, "Reckless Love of God" chorus)."

Respond to the Lord about what He's shown you today.

DAY THREE STUDY

Read 2 Chronicles 32:1-23. Ask the Lord Jesus to speak to you through His Word. Tell Him that you are listening. Optional: Read Isaiah 36-39.

Hezekiah led the greatest revival in Israel's history. He worshiped God with his heart, mind, and body just like David had done. But monster-size trouble is on its way. The "monster" Assyria was the most feared nation in the ancient world at the time of Hezekiah and for good reason. They built roads wide enough for their wheeled vehicles and their armies to move quickly to wherever they were needed. And the Assyrians were very brutal with those they conquered. To the people of Judah, the threat and their fear were real, not imaginary. They needed God's perspective.

Historical Insight: The biblical account of Sennacherib's attacks on Judah (701 BC) correspond very closely with Sennacherib's own account. In his annals, Sennacherib claims to have captured 46 of Hezekiah's fortified cities, as well as numerous open villages, and to have taken 200,146 of the people captive. He says he made Hezekiah "a prisoner in Jerusalem his royal residence, like a bird in a cage," but he does not say he took Jerusalem. (*NIV Study Bible 1985 Edition,* note on 2 Kings 18:13, p. 559)

10. Focus on vv. 1-8. This event occurred in Hezekiah's 14th year of being king (age 39).

- What happened in v. 1, and why does that seem to go against our way of thinking?

- How did Hezekiah prepare for the defense of Jerusalem (vv. 2-8)?

11. Focus on vv. 9-19. Discuss the propaganda campaign of Sennacherib and his officers through letters and speeches—the purpose, lies, twisting of truth, etc.

12. Isaiah wrote about this incident and more in Isaiah chapters 36-39. Read Isaiah 37:1-7, 14-38.

  - How did Hezekiah respond to the letter sent from Sennacherib (vv. 1 and 14)?

  - What poured out of Hezekiah's heart to the Lord (vv. 15-20)?

  - What were the main points of God's message back to Sennacherib (vv. 21-35)?

  - How did God deliver Jerusalem from the danger (vv. 36-37)?

  - How did God avenge the evil acts of Sennacherib against His people (v. 38)? See also 2 Chronicles 32:21.

13. Read 2 Chronicles 32:24-33 and Isaiah 38:1-8. Discuss what happened right after the deliverance from Assyria's clutches.

14. ***Deeper Discoveries (optional):*** Read Isaiah 38:1-39:8.

- What did Hezekiah learn from his illness (vv. 15-20)?

- What did God use to heal him (v. 21)?

- What test did God give to Hezekiah in 39:1-8 and how did the king respond to the test and the results?

The account of Hezekiah's response to Sennacherib's attack on Jerusalem is an illustration of the two aspects of trusting God.

1) You must trust Him as you step forward and do your part His way. Hezekiah took necessary preparations for defending his city and people as God would want him as a leader to do.

2) You must trust God to do His part in the areas over which you have no control. Hezekiah brought the letter before the Lord, asked Him to intervene, and trusted God to do that.

Those two aspects of trusting God are necessary to act on whatever God has placed in your heart to do or for any situation where you find yourself threatened.

15. ***Reboot, renew, rejoice:*** Has God allowed a threatening situation into your life? It could be correcting sinful behavior or speaking up in a situation where a voice with biblical principles needs to be heard. It could be facing a lawsuit with courage and peace. Whatever it is still involves the two aspects of trusting God. Considering your situation,

- How are you trusting Him as you step forward to do your part His way? What common sense / realistic preparations can you take?

- How are you trusting Him to do His part in the areas over which you have no control? What have you placed in His hands? Where the Word of God is clear, you can claim God's promises by faith. Anytime, you can ask, but you cannot hold God to promises He hasn't made.

Think About It: Outcomes in this life are unpredictable. The person of faith says, "God's will be done. I'm in His hands," trusts in Him, and walks ahead. (Tim Stevenson)

Respond to the Lord about what He's shown you today.

DAY FOUR STUDY

Read 2 Chronicles 33:1-20. Ask the Lord Jesus to speak to you through His Word. Tell Him that you are listening.

> **Scriptural Insight:** Based on 2 Kings 21:1, we know that Manasseh was born after Hezekiah's illness.

16. How did Manasseh undo all of his father's hard work (vv. 2-9)?

> **Think About It:** Does it surprise you that the people went along with this after their religious reboot under Hezekiah?

17. What did God do to get Manasseh's attention (vv. 10-11)? See also 2 Kings 21:10-15.

18. How did Manasseh respond (2 Chronicles 33:12-17)?

> **Focus on the Meaning:** Chronicles teaches us that God is bigger than our past. Each generation has the opportunity—and the responsibility—to repent and turn to God for blessing. And even our own personal history of sin is not enough to stop God's grace. The Chronicler shows us the repentance of David and Hezekiah, and even the worst king of all, Manasseh, turns to God and is forgiven. And the biggest reverse of all is that even the tragedy of the exile to Babylon is not the end of God's plans for His people. God forgives His people and brings them back to the land. If you are someone who is tempted to think that your past will make God give up on you, Chronicles can be a constant reminder of **the unstoppable power of God's forgiveness.** (James Duguid, "Why Study the Books of 1-2 Chronicles?" crossway.org)

Manasseh's son Amon became the next king. He only reigned two years and did the evil that his father modeled for him. Manasseh's reboot came too late to benefit his son. *"Unlike his father Manasseh, he did not humble himself before the Lord"* (2 Chronicles 33:23.)

19. ***Reboot, renew, rejoice:*** Manasseh's example should give hope to anyone who trusts in Christ after years of going against Him. What do you learn about God's grace to anyone who chooses repentance—turning away from rebellion against Him, choosing to acknowledge His sovereignty instead? Is it ever too late for anyone still living?

20. ***Reboot, renew, rejoice:*** There are two examples of repentance in this lesson. Manasseh's repentance turned from total unbelief to belief in God. His life was completely rebooted. Hezekiah's example is that of dealing with recognized sin in your life. As long as you live in your earthly body, sin will happen—whether intentionally or unintentionally. And though our God is no longer counting our sins against us (2 Corinthians 5:19), we still must deal with the consequences of any sinful behavior.

Addressing recognized sin in your life is part of living dependently on the Lord. Whenever the Spirit convicts you of thinking or behavior that is definitely not pleasing to the Lord, you can this biblical process to deal with it:

- **Step One: View yourself rightly.** Your identity is not "_____" (coveter, greedy, gossiper, whatever the sin is).

    You are in Christ, a child of God, who sometimes "_____" (covets, is greedy, gossips).

- **Step Two: Recognize (confess) the truth regarding your sin.** To confess biblically means *to agree with God about what you and He both know to be true.* Confession is not a formula, a process, or dependent on a mediator. Regarding sin in your life, it is not saying, "I'm sorry." It is saying, "I agree with you, God. I blew it!" You see your sin as awful!

    Using sexual immorality as an example: while reading 1 Thessalonians 4:1-8, the Spirit convicts you that sexual immorality in any form is not pleasing to God. You are instructed to "flee/avoid immorality." You recognize this sin in your life. You agree with God that your immoral sexual behavior is seeking love and acceptance from the wrong source. It doesn't fit someone who knows God. That is confession.

- **Step Three: Confession is incomplete without repentance.** Repentance means *to change your mind about that sin, to mourn its ugliness, resulting in changing your actions.* Paul calls that godly sorrow in 2 Corinthians 7:9-11, and he says godly sorrow produces repentance. It's saying, "I recognize what I am doing is wrong. This fills me with sorrow because it displeases You, God. Please help me to live differently." He will certainly do that! That's how our lives get transformed.

    For sexual immorality: You want to live in order to please God, and God wants you to avoid sexual immorality. So, you pray, "Lord Jesus, please have your Spirit nudge me when I am not holy and honorable with my body. Help me to say no to temptation and to give up any relationship that is not honorable to you. By faith, Lord, I want you to do that in my life." That is repentance.

- **Step Four: Repentance leads to dependence.** Depend on the living Christ inside you for that change to take place. Our Lord Jesus Christ is not interested in our compliance (outward conformity) as much as He desires our *obedience* from the heart. And trust in Him to help you overcome the consequences of any sinful choices you have made in a way that brings glory to Him.

> *For sexual immorality: Memorize 1 Thessalonians 4:1-8 and any other scriptures that deal with staying pure and not rejecting God's instructions. Be sensitive to the Spirit's nudging when you are tempted to do otherwise. Choose to desire a life that pleases God.*

Follow this process for dealing with any recognized sin in your life today.

REBOOT RENEW REJOICE

21. What is your one take-away from Lesson 10?

Our God's powerful presence helps us to reboot our lives, renew our commitment to Him, and live a life of rejoicing as a result.

Respond to the Lord about what He's shown you today.

Recommended: Listen to the podcast "The Unstoppable Power of God's Forgiveness" after doing this lesson to reinforce what you have learned. Use the following listener guide.

The Unstoppable Power of God's Forgiveness

When your judgments [God] come upon the earth, the people of the world learn righteousness. But when grace is shown to the wicked, they do not learn righteousness; even in a land of uprightness they go on doing evil and do not regard the majesty of the Lord." (Isaiah 26:9-10)

FEAR OF CONSEQUENCES LED TO REPENTANCE AND RENEWAL

- Hezekiah's first priority after becoming king was to repair and reopen the Temple, which had been ravaged and shuttered by his father. It was time for a fresh start, a reboot of Judah as a nation under God.

- After 16 days of cleansing, Hezekiah called together all the local leaders and publicly led them to repentance of their past sins and renewal of their commitment to God.

- Hezekiah invited all the people in his land plus those Jews left behind in the northern kingdom to come to Jerusalem to celebrate the Passover. This was an attempt to unite Israel into one nation again after 215 years of separation. Some in the north scorned and ridiculed the couriers and the message as people do today. But many people humbled themselves and went to Jerusalem. That's repentance.

- Hezekiah prayed for God's grace upon the people who really didn't remember how to purify themselves. Our gracious God heard Hezekiah and cleansed the people. God has always responded to repentance with His mercy and grace. Gentiles in the assembly were accepted by God that day by faith—a foreshadowing of the future Church of Jesus Christ.

REPENTANCE AND RENEWAL LED TO ACTION

- The people acted out their heart change by smashing the idols and places of idol worship throughout both the southern kingdom and what was left of the northern kingdom to do the same. Humility before God leads to obedience to God. Fear of the consequences of continuing their wicked lifestyle (the threat of captivity and exile) motivated their humility and obedience. A heart change leads to a life change.

- God gave us fear as a gift. Fear is a normal human emotion designed by God to alert us to danger so we will take action against it. This is present even in the first command given to humans in Genesis 2:16-17. Because of His love, God gave the women of Jerusalem a 1-year advance warning of what was going to happen so they would reboot their hearts. *Isaiah 32:9-10*

- God sent many prophets wooing the people back to God. They spurned His grace and His love and His protection.

- But His love for them didn't end. God gave the people a leader. Hezekiah did what was good and right and faithful before the Lord. It's much better to approach life God's way. A healthy fear of consequences can motivate selfish people to follow God instead.

- Hezekiah did make some sinful choices in his life as we all do, even those of us who are walking with God daily. But his overall walk with God was faithful. He connected with his people, and they benefited under his authority.

THE DISCONNECTED LEADER

- Hezekiah's son Manasseh ignored the prophets and chose to follow the pattern of his wicked grandfather Ahaz rather than what was modeled before him in his godly father Hezekiah.

- Not only was Manasseh a horribly wicked leader for his people, leading them back to idolatry, his practices were more wicked than any of the surrounding pagan nations!

- There are always consequences to wicked behavior. And God uses those consequences to encourage repentance.

THE UNSTOPPABLE POWER OF GOD'S FORGIVENESS

- God used Manasseh's humiliating imprisonment by the Assyrians to Babylon to capture Manasseh's attention! He went back to Jerusalem a changed man and did the right things in God's eyes. *2 Chronicles 33:12-13*

- Each one of us comes to God on our own merits not on our parents' merits. Even those raised in ungodly homes can learn to love God well and break the wicked cycle.

  If you are someone who is tempted to think that your past will make God give up on you, Chronicles can be a constant reminder of **the unstoppable power of God's forgiveness.** (James Duguid, "Why Study the Books of 1-2 Chronicles?" www.crossway.org)

As believers in Jesus Christ, we have God's continual forgiveness for every sin—past, present, and future. But even more than that, we have the power of God's presence with us. Our God's powerful presence helps us to reboot our lives, renew our commitment to Him, and live a life of rejoicing as a result. What a blessing!

Let Jesus satisfy your heart with the power of His presence. Then, live in that power!

11 A Hope and a Future

2 Chronicles 34-36; Ezra 1 (640-516 BC)

DAY ONE STUDY

Historical Perspective

With the fall of the Northern Kingdom, Judah remained alone. She had been able to escape an early ruin because the Davidic dynasty remained stable and several of Judah's kings were godly leaders for their people, doing "what was right in the eyes of the Lord."

Also, God sent zealous prophets to exhort Judah to love and obey God. Isaiah, Micah, Zephaniah, Habakkuk, and Jeremiah poured out God's appeals for repentance and faith upon Judah. Wicked kings, however, like Ahaz and Manasseh damaged the moral fiber of the people. The idolatrous worship of foreign gods (Baal and Molech especially) remained a temptation.

But God always preserves a remnant for Himself of faithful believers. And to that remnant, He gives hope for living through the rough-and-tumble of real life as well as hope for the future. As it did for the Israelites, history can be a call to worship and invitation to hope. When you remember times that God blessed you, acted on your behalf, and carried you through a rough time, such memories are blessings in themselves as well as encouragement to press on in holiness and confidence in God.

> **Think About It:** A prayer journal that recalls prayers asked and those answered can act as your own "history" manual. God wants us to remember His works, so we, too, can praise Him for His goodness and have hope for our future. (Chuck Swindoll, *Second Chronicles Overview*, insight.org)

Read 2 Chronicles 34:1-13. Ask the Lord Jesus to speak to you through His Word. Tell Him that you are listening.

1. What do you learn about Josiah's early years (vv. 1-7)? See also 2 Kings 23:4-20 for more details.

> **Think About It:** Josiah had faith as a child despite his wicked father. Maybe he had a great mother. Hilkiah the High Priest was evidently a strong influence in his life. As a 16-year-old, he sought a deeper relationship with God. I've seen that happen in teens and young adults when they turn the childhood faith they got from their parents into a personal faith for themselves. Have you? By the time he turned 20, he was ready to act as a godly leader for his people—purging Judah and Jerusalem of idolatry.

2. What work did he undertake in his 20's (2 Chronicles 34:8-13)?

> **Historical Insight:** Interestingly, most of the reformations and return to worshiping the Lord started at the Temple. Asa, Jehoshaphat, Joash, and Hezekiah repaired and restored worship at the Temple early in their reigns as king. People were drawn to the Temple to renew their commitment to God and then take that renewal back to their communities to continue.

Read 2 Chronicles 34:14-33.

3. Sometimes when you do some deep cleaning, you get a surprise. That's what happened here. Hilkiah the priest found "the Book of the Law of the LORD that had been given through Moses." This is either the books of Exodus through Deuteronomy or just the book of Deuteronomy.

    • When Josiah heard the words of the Law read, what did he do (vv. 19-21)?

    • To whom did Hilkiah go to inquire of the Lord?

> **Focus on the Meaning:** Throughout Israel's history, God raised up women to speak for Him as prophets. Miriam, Deborah, and Huldah are three of the best-known ones. Huldah lived in Jerusalem and was married to the grandson of someone who served in the king's palace taking care of his royal robes. The High Priest Hilkiah already knew of Huldah's reputation as a prophet of the Lord and had no hesitation in seeking Huldah's counsel from the Lord. Nor did Josiah hesitate in obeying the Word of the Lord given to him through Huldah.

    • Discuss the response from the Lord that she gave them (vv. 23-28).

- What did Josiah do after getting God's answer (vv. 29-33)? See also 2 Kings 23:24.

God's answer through the prophetess Huldah spurred Josiah to bring the people together so he could read God's Word to them. Don't you love that? After reading it, he renewed the covenant with God for himself then had the people do it for themselves. That's a good leader. As long as he lived, the people obeyed God. Leadership makes such a difference to the direction people take.

4. Read the following verses. What information is given about the impact of hearing or reading God's Word?

    - Isaiah 55:10-11—

    - Hebrews 4:12—

    - 2 Timothy 3:16-17—

5. ***Reboot, renew, rejoice:*** Do you remember a time when you discovered something new in the Word of the Lord that wowed, humbled, encouraged, or rebuked you? What about in this study? Write about that here and share with someone this week what you learned.

Respond to the Lord about what He's shown you today.

DAY TWO STUDY

Read 2 Chronicles 35:1-19. Ask the Lord Jesus to speak to you through His Word. Tell Him that you are listening.

Passover commemorated Israel's redemption from Egyptian slavery and was the greatest feast. The day of Passover was followed by 7 more days of celebration called the Feast of Unleavened Bread.

6.   What grabbed your attention when you read this passage?

Scriptural Insight: Apparently from v. 3, the ark of the Covenant had been removed from the Temple, perhaps for protection during the evil reigns of Manasseh and Amon. When the Babylonians destroyed the Temple 30 years later, there was no mention of the ark of the Covenant among the treasures brought to Babylon. Nor was it mentioned among the objects returned to Jerusalem by Cyrus, king of Persia, years later. None of the prophets mentioned its whereabouts. It was not mentioned in the second Temple built by the returning exiles. Even the New Testament makes no mention of the ark of the Covenant within the Temple. The ark completely disappeared from history. In Revelation 11:19, though, John sees the ark in a vision of God's Temple in heaven. Have you wondered (as I have) why it just wasn't remade along with all the other furnishings when the new Temple was built by the returning exiles?

Read 2 Chronicles 35: 20-36:1.

Pharaoh Neco was on his way to the Euphrates River (modern Iraq) to help the king of Assyria fight against the king of Babylon (609 BC). The Assyrian capital had already fallen to the Babylonians whose army was led by Nebuchadnezzar. The highway to get to the Euphrates went right through the western portion of Judah.

7.   Discuss the message that Pharaoh Neco sent to Josiah (v. 21).

8.   What choice did Josiah make and at what cost (vv. 22-24)?

Think About It: Josiah adopted Ahab's practice from 250 years earlier. Did he not think God could be consulted about this? Did he feel it to be his duty as king to engage Neco? Had he grown prideful or too confident in his success as had Uzziah? Did he not think God could speak truth through a pagan king?

9. Read 2 Kings 23:25-27.

   - What do you learn from verses 25 and 26?

   - What decision had God already made (2 Chronicles 34:23-28)?

10. How could the reforms and recommitment to God that happened under Josiah's leadership have benefited those Jews who were captured and brought to pagan Babylon just a few years later?

The privileged "chosen" were taken to Babylon. Their lives were ripped up and overturned. They were immersed in a culture alien to their faith. They had a few options: 1) Rebel and die. 2) Surrender to despair. 3) Compromise and conform to survive and succeed. 4) Submit and compromise as far as possible within limits set by Scripture, while maintaining by faith a firm identity and integrity. Many chose option 4 because of Josiah's leadership renewing and strengthening their faith in and reliance on God. Among those are Daniel, Shadrach, Meshach, and Abednego. You can read their stories of how they did it in the book of Daniel.

11. ***Reboot, renew, rejoice:*** What have you done in your faith walk with the Lord that will benefit or have benefited those who come after you?

Respond to the Lord about what He's shown you today.

DAY THREE STUDY

Read 2 Chronicles 36:1-14. Ask the Lord Jesus to speak to you through His Word. Tell Him that you are listening.

12. Josiah's sons became pawns between the Pharaoh Neco and the king of Babylon. Like choosing sides for a sports team, you need a scorecard. I've provided one for you in a chart below. Why is this important? God promised to maintain a descendant of David eligible for the throne. We will see how He did that in all the chaos.

From the verses you just read, look at the chart below. Notice how God in His grace preserved David's royal line. Circle the one that continues it.

	Josiah's descendants	
Son #1: Jehoahaz (vv. 1-4) After 3 months of being king, he was taken to Egypt where he died without heirs.	*Son #2: Eliakim (aka Jehoiakim, vv. 5-8)*—He died in Jerusalem before he could be taken to Babylon. His son *Jehoiachin (vv. 9-10)* was taken to Babylon, and his descendants carried on the line of David (1 Chronicles 3:17).	*Son #3: Mattaniah (aka Zedekiah, vv. 11-14)* After a long time of resisting surrender, he was captured, blinded, and all his sons were killed. He was taken to Babylon without heirs.

13. ***Deeper Discoveries (optional):*** The prophet Habakkuk wrote during the time of Babylon's threat to Jerusalem. Habakkuk is someone who remained faithful to God, perhaps influenced by the godly leadership of Josiah as he grew up. Now, he questions why God is permitting the wickedness to go on in Jerusalem. Read the 3 chapters to see God's answer and Habakkuk's response.

Read 2 Chronicles 36:15-21.

14. Let's look at what is revealed in 2 Chronicles 36:15-21 from God's perspective.

- What do you learn from vv. 15-16?

- What did God allow to happen (vv. 17-21)? [Optional: for more details, you can read 2 Kings 25:1-26.]

Scriptural Insight: Through Jeremiah the prophet, God offered Zedekiah the opportunity to save Jerusalem from being burned and his family from being destroyed by the Babylonian commander Nebuchadnezzar (Jeremiah 38:14-28). All he had to do was surrender. Zedekiah's response was not to accept God's mercy and grace through obeying Him and doing it God's way. Instead, Zedekiah chose to protect himself and listen to his peers, to ignore the conflict, and hope it would go away. It didn't. His family was killed in front of him, he was blinded, and Jerusalem was burned, including the Temple. Why wasn't the Temple saved? For 500 years, Solomon's Temple had stood to remind the people that God ruled over their nation. Yet, it had become a hollow symbol of religious practice rather than a celebration of the presence of God and the relationship anyone could have with Him. God was more interested in the hearts of His people than any elaborate building. He still is!

15. God, in His love, sent Jeremiah, Zephaniah, and Habakkuk as speaking and writing prophets to Judah during this time period.

- What other details are given in Jeremiah 25:8-12?

- What is the promise in Jeremiah 27:22?

Historical Insight: There were actually several different times during this period (607-586 BC) when the Jews were taken captive by Babylon. In 607 BC, Nebuchadnezzar took many of the finest and brightest young men from each city in Judah captive, including Daniel and his three friends. Nine years later (598 BC), Nebuchadnezzar laid siege to Jerusalem, taking captive almost all of the population of Judah, leaving only the poorest people of the land. Twelve years later (586 BC), the majority of the Jewish people were taken captive, but Nebuchadnezzar again left the remnant of poor people to serve as farmers and vinedressers in the land. The 70 years ended in 537 BC. God said in Jeremiah 27:22 and 29:10 that He would come for them. And He did!

16. **Deeper Discoveries (optional):** The book of Jeremiah is like reading a personal journal of his experience during this time as well as a historical record of God's communication with the people and their response to Him, including all of Josiah's sons and grandson. It's a long read, but you might find it more understandable when you read it in the context of what you have learned in the study of 2 Chronicles 34-36.

17. In His love for His people, God sent a letter written by Jeremiah to those initially taken as exiles into Babylon and those taken ten years later. Read Jeremiah 29:1-14. What instruction and encouragement does He give them so they can function well and take advantage of that time they will be there?

Focus on the Meaning: Jeremiah 29:11 is often quoted out of context, finding its way onto wall decorations, note cards, and pillows. In context, the promise would not be fulfilled until after the 70 years of exile. During that long time of waiting, they were to function well, doing those things in life that would benefit themselves and those around them. When God was ready to reboot Israel, they needed to be ready mentally, physically, skillfully, and spiritually for the reboot.

18. *Reboot, renew, rejoice:* Looking at Jeremiah 29:1-14, how do you take those words from God about how to function well in a difficult time of waiting and apply them to your life? What can you do now to prepare yourself for the next stage of your life?

Respond to the Lord about what He's shown you today.

DAY FOUR STUDY

As a review, this is what happened so far in chapter 36. After only 3 months of being king, Josiah's son Jehoahaz was deposed by Pharaoh Neco and taken captive to Egypt. Neco then placed his older brother Eliakim on the throne and changed his name to Jehoiakim. As a pawn of Egypt, Jehoiakim was the "king" of Judah for 11 years. Then, Babylon took charge of Judah so Nebuchadnezzar took Jehoiakim captive to Babylon along with a bunch of Temple treasures then put Jehoiakim's son Jehoiachin on the throne. After only 3 months, Jehoiachin was taken to Babylon along with more Temple treasures. Do you see a pattern here? Who would have willingly raised his hand next to become king? Not me! Well, Nebuchadnezzar chose Josiah's son Mattaniah (who would have been about 6 when his father died) and gave him the name Zedekiah.

The prophet Jeremiah was actively bringing God's Word throughout the 11 years Zedekiah was on the throne. Through one specific message (Jeremiah 38:14-28), God offered to spare Zedekiah, his family, and the whole city of Jerusalem from destruction if Zedekiah would simply surrender to Nebuchadnezzar. He could have saved the lives of many people and the Temple from being destroyed! But he refused to follow Jeremiah's counsel! Zedekiah "became stiff-necked and hardened his heart and would not turn to the Lord. Furthermore, all the leaders of the priests and the people became more and more unfaithful following all the detestable practices of the nations" (2 Chronicles 36:13-14). Zedekiah ended up being blinded, his family killed in front of him, the city ravaged and the Temple completely destroyed.

But God had a plan for his people. Within 20 years of Josiah's death, the evil cancer of idolatry had returned. God cleaned up the filth. The wicked and unrepentant died at the hands of Nebuchadnezzar while those whose hearts were teachable were taken captive to Babylon for 70 years. Second Chronicles concludes with the decree of Cyrus after the 70-year captivity with no record of the captivity itself. The only records we have of this time are the books of Jeremiah, Daniel, and Ezekiel.

The exiled Judeans were treated with some measure of respect in Babylon. Some became prosperous businessmen. Others rose to political power (Daniel and his friends). The prophets Daniel and Jeremiah held out hope for Israel's return according to God's promise.

Read 2 Chronicles 36:21-23. Ask the Lord Jesus to speak to you through His Word. Tell Him that you are listening.

19. God kept His promise to His people. What happened after the 70 years of exile ended?

Read Ezra 1:1-8. Ezra covers the time period of the return of the exiles back to their homeland and the reboot of their religious life.

> **Scriptural Insight:** Ezra was a priest and a scribe, one who "had devoted himself to the study and observance of the Law of the Lord (Ezra 7:10)." Ezra led a group of exiles from Babylon to Judah 80 years after the first group returned. The books of Ezra and Nehemiah are actually one book in the Hebrew Bible and contain eyewitness accounts written by the two principal characters.

20. What additional information about Cyrus is given in vv. 1-4? Review Jeremiah 27:22.

21. What followed the decree (vv. 5-8)?

Read Ezra 2:1. Skim 2:36-54 then read 61-70.

22. You now see the need for 1 Chronicles chapters 1-9. Discuss what they needed to know about their heritage as they rebooted their homeland.

> **Scriptural Insight:** By tracing the history of God's people, the author of the Chronicles reminded the new generation that God had been their help in ages past. By emphasizing the unconditional Davidic Covenant, he gave them hope for the future. By including the genealogies, he showed them that they were the ones to continue the legacy. In short, the author of the Chronicles showed a despairing people that they had a powerful, faithful God who would strengthen them to rebuild the Temple and the city. ("What is the purpose of First and Second Chronicles?" Gotquestions.org)

23. Read 1 Chronicles 3:16-19. God in His faithfulness preserved the line of David through Jehoiachin. Put the name of Jehoiachin's son Shealtiel in the chart below where it belongs (*Great-Grandson*).

Josiah's descendants
Son #2: Eliakim (aka Jehoiakim)
Grandson: Jehoiachin (brought to Babylon)
Great-Grandson:
Next descendant:

24. Look at Matthew 1:6-13. Find Jehoiachin, Shealtiel and Zerubbabel in the lineage of Joseph. Zerubbabel was either Shealtiel's son, nephew, or grandson. Put his name in the chart as *next descendant*. Through this lineage (and that of Mary in Luke 3:27), Jesus was the rightful

heir to the throne of Israel. Note: Jeconiah and Jehoiachin are different spellings of the same person.

25. Read Ezra 2:2 and 3:1-9. Jeshua (Hebrew, "the Lord saves") was the High Priest. Zerubbabel (recognized to be in the line of David) was appointed governor of Judah (known as "Transjordan") by the Persian king. As governor, how did he participate in the reboot of Israel?

God sent the prophets Haggai and Zechariah to encourage and support Zerubbabel during the building of the second Temple. The Lord God was pleased with Zerubbabel's efforts in returning the captives to Jerusalem, in building the second Temple, and in reestablishing the Temple worship. With God's prompting, Haggai gave Zerubbabel a special blessing:

> *"On that day," declares the LORD Almighty, "I will take you, my servant Zerubbabel son of Shealtiel," declares the LORD, "and I will make you like my signet ring, for I have chosen you,' declares the LORD Almighty." (Haggai 2:23)*

The temple was completed almost 70 years after its destruction. Older Jews who recalled the size and grandeur of the first Temple wept as they compared Zerubbabel's Temple (smaller and with less glitz) to the splendor of Solomon's Temple. Also, Solomon's Temple had housed the ark of the Covenant, which was apparently no longer in Israel's possession. At the first temple's dedication, the altar had been lit by fire from heaven, and the Temple had been filled with the Shekinah glory. There is no record of such a miracle at the second Temple's dedication. Haggai prophesied that the second Temple would one day have a magnificence to outshine the glory of the first (Haggai 2:3–9). God's promise was fulfilled 500 years later when the Messiah Himself (Jesus Christ) walked the courts of the Temple that Zerubbabel built (and King Herod later refurbished). Jesus confirmed that God dwelled in the second Temple (Matthew 23:21).

During the 70 years of captivity, the Jews learned to trust God alone and give up any idolatrous tendencies. After the 70 years, the faithful were allowed to return to rebuild the Temple in Jerusalem and their homeland. A revival among Jews took place after the return of the Jews to Israel and the rebuilding of the Temple. We see those accounts in Ezra and Nehemiah accompanied with lots of rejoicing.

God's steadfast love brought back a remnant of faithful Jews to regain their land and their purpose to once again be a light for the Gentiles. A reboot. Israel would never again participate in the idolatry and worship of false gods of the surrounding nations. Israel clung to their God for the next few hundred years, thus preparing them for the coming of their Messiah. I would have given up on such a stiff-necked people. God didn't. Thankfully in His steadfast love, He is still wooing those whose hearts are pliable towards Him.

REBOOT RENEW REJOICE

26. What is your one take-away from Lesson 11?

27. What have you learned in this study of Chronicles about God's faithfulness to you in giving you the opportunity to reboot your life through faith in Christ?

Our God's powerful presence helps us to reboot our lives, renew our commitment to Him, and live a life of rejoicing as a result.

Respond to the Lord about what He's shown you today.

> **Recommended:** Listen to the podcast "God's Steadfast Love Leads to Reboot and Renewal" after doing this lesson to reinforce what you have learned. Use the following listener guide.

God's Steadfast Love Leads to Reboot and Renewal

In the Protestant Reformation, God chose to use ordinary people who were His faithful followers to reboot the Church of Jesus Christ. They returned to what was clearly preached in the New Testament that salvation is by grace alone through faith alone. Good works result from our faith but are not the grounds for our right standing before God. God declares that we are forgiven of sin and righteous in His sight through our faith alone. And the Scriptures have authority over tradition.

But all of this change came about because the faithful endured God's painful pruning of the Church. God weeded out those who were not His and preserved a remnant of faithful Christians who were wholeheartedly committed to Him. They and their descendants changed the world.

GOD'S STEADFAST LOVE SHOWN TO JOSIAH

- Israel's purpose was to represent God on earth and proclaim His glory and holiness to the pagan nations around them. But the people chose wickedness. That wickedness demanded that God take action. God's wrath cleans and restores. Stiff-necked humans let themselves get absolutely filthy, polluting God's creation. But God's love provides a way for those who want to get cleaned up and restored to their purpose. *Isaiah 26:9-10*

- Young Josiah must have had a child-like faith in spite of his wicked father. At age 16, he began to seek God. In his 20s, he acted as a godly leader for his people—purging Judah and Jerusalem of idolatry and renewing their covenant with God. He did what was right in the eyes of the Lord and what was right for his people. As long as he lived, the people obeyed God.

GOD STEADFAST LOVE PURIFIES HIS PEOPLE

- Several of Josiah's sons were placed on the throne, one by Pharaoh and two by Nebuchadnezzar, the king of Babylon. All four of them did evil in God's eyes. The last one was Zedekiah, a puppet king of Nebuchadnezzar. But God was still sovereign.

- Jeremiah the prophet brought God's Word throughout Zedekiah's 11 years. Zedekiah refused God's offer of protection for him, his family, and Jerusalem. *Jeremiah 38:17-18*

- Within 20 years of Josiah's death, the evil cancer of idolatry had returned. God had to clean up the filth and purify His people! God's discipline of Israel had a purpose.
  - ✓ The wicked and unrepentant died at the hands of Nebuchadnezzar.
  - ✓ Those whose hearts were pliable were taken captive to Babylon for 70 years. There, they learned to trust God alone and give up any idolatrous behavior.
  - ✓ After the 70 years, the faithful were allowed to return to rebuild the Temple in Jerusalem and their homeland.
- God's steadfast love brought back faithful Jews to regain their land and their purpose to once again be a light for the Gentiles. Israel clung to their God for the next few hundred years, thus preparing them for the coming of their Messiah. *Isaiah 55:8-12*

GOD'S STEADFAST LOVE PLANNED FOR THE FUTURE

God caused the destruction of Jerusalem and the Temple to work for good for His people in a way that eventually benefited you and me.

- Captive in Babylon, cut off from the Temple, and surrounded by pagan religious practices, the Jews concentrated on what they had—their God and the Torah (the first five books of the Bible). While they were in exile, they kept their identity as God's people and learned how to live out their faith through personal piety and prayer rather than the sacrifices that were no longer available to them. The center of worship became something new—the local synagogue. As a result, Judaism became a faith that could be practiced wherever the Jews could meet and the Torah could be read.

- The dispersion of Israel (the Diaspora) that began with the exile accelerated during the years that followed so that by the time of Jesus, Jews filled every land in the Middle East. This prepared the way for the Christian gospel. The missionaries of the early church began their Gentile ministries among the Diaspora, in their synagogues, using the Greek translation of the Old Testament that nearly everyone could read. Within many Jewish synagogue congregations were "God-fearing" Gentiles—the non-Jews who believed in the Jewish God and followed the Law to some extent.

- After the exile, a religious group formed to keep Israel pure from idolatry. They did this by promoting the keeping of the Law as the only way that the Jews would be able to live righteously before God in a world that had changed drastically since the days of Moses. We know them in the Gospels as the Pharisees. They had helped to make sure Israel was mostly idol-free in preparation for the coming of Jesus Christ.

- When Jesus came to earth, the power of God's presence was manifested in a very personal way. As Tony Evans says, Jesus is God's selfie. Jesus said, "When you look at me, you see the Father." He lived His life in dependence on God so that we would know how to do that too. Jesus gave His life for us on the cross so that we could become new creatures with complete forgiveness of our sins and a reconciled relationship with our God. Jesus rose from the dead so that He could give His life to us through the Holy Spirit that lives inside of every believer. And because of the power of God's presence in us, Jesus can live His life through us.

Dear reader, be like the men and women of the Reformation. Take the truths of Scripture to heart. Come to God and be saved by His grace alone through your faith alone. Commit your life to following Him, renewing that commitment every day. And rejoice because of what He has done and is doing in your life. Our God's powerful presence helps you to do that!

Let Jesus satisfy your heart with the power of His presence. Then, live in that power!

Map of the Twelve Tribes

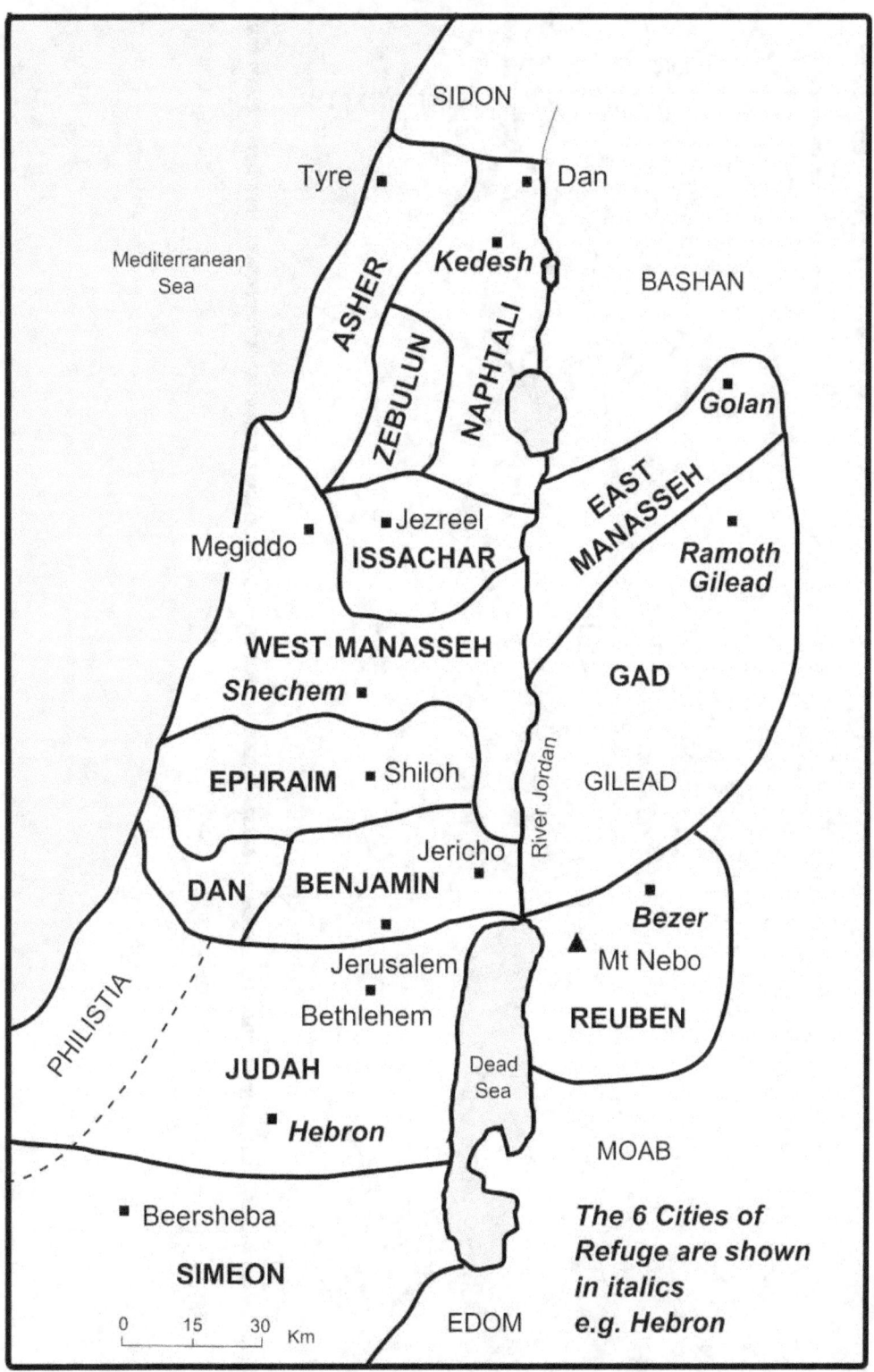

This is Map 49: "The Boundaries of the Twelve Tribes," accessed from thebiblejourney.org.

Map of the Kingdoms of Israel and Judah

This is the 1994 version of this map originally found at bible.ca, accessed from paradisepbc.org.

Small Group Discussion Guide

The following guide is designed for groups that meet for about 1½ hours or less. You will notice that some questions are skipped for the sake of time.

INTRODUCTION TO STUDY

It is not necessary to have a separate week for introducing the study. It can be a good time to get to know one another and give them a vision for the whole study. Send the podcast link beforehand.

- Start with prayer. Pray for the group to learn from Jesus what He wants them to know and to learn to love one another well to build your community.

- Make sure everyone has a book, a schedule, and Bible / Bible app and knows how to use it. Ask if anyone is new to the Bible and plan to come alongside her during the week.

- Get acquainted with each other. Ask a general question or two such as, "Share your name, where you live, and an activity you enjoy when you have time to do so."

Introduce the study

- Pray: Ask Jesus to teach you through this study what He wants you to know.

- Look at the "Contents" page to see the lesson titles.

- Introduction Page 1. Read the top paragraphs and "The Basic Study" section. Draw their attention to the useful study tools given.

- Tell them how to find the podcasts (melanienewton.com/podcasts or any podcast platform—search "Satisfied" by Melanie Newton, Season 6: 1 & 2 Chronicles). Use the QR code for quick access. Or they can read the associated blogs at melanienewton.com/blog (1 & 2 Chronicles category).

- Ask: Who has good knowledge of Old Testament history? There is an Old Testament Summary and Timeline on page 2. There are two maps at the end of the book that will help you during the study to get your geographic bearings.

- Read the paragraph at the top of page 3.

- Say: Be assured that God is the same God in the Old Testament and New Testament. He extended grace and mercy to Old Testament people who received eternal life by faith in God. For Jews, their earthly life was managed by the Mosaic Law given to Israel. Its purpose was to lead people to faith in God, devotion to God, and a relationship with God.

- Read "Discussion Group Guidelines." Add anything else pertinent to your group.

A Fresh Start podcast

- Read and discuss the listener guide on pages 9-10. Ask questions based on your notes from listening to the podcast ahead of time.

- Discuss the reboot of Israel in 1948AD and the reboot of Israel after the exile in 537BC. Discuss the meanings and occasions for someone to reboot, renew, and how they rejoice. Read 2 Chronicles 36:15-21 to see what happened to cause the reboot. Read the theme statement at the end together.

Other

- Remind them to do Lesson 1 for next meeting. Pray.

LESSON 1: AN UNBROKEN CONNECTION

Each lesson in this study covers several chapters. Choose ahead of time which verses from the questions the group will read aloud as you proceed through the discussion. My recommendations are below. Remind them to listen to the podcasts beforehand.

Start with prayer. If this is first week, ask what grabbed their attention from the introductory podcast.

Day One

- Qs 1 & 2. Optional: Show family pictures.

Day Two

- "Reboot": Read "Focus on the Meaning." Highlight meaning of "reboot."

- Q3: Ask what they learned from those verses. Read the next paragraph.

- Q4: Ask what they learned from those verses.

- "Renew": Read the second paragraph.

- Q5: Ask what they learned from those verses about renewing your faith walk.

- "Rejoice": Read the paragraph. Q6: Ask what they learned from those verses.

- Skip "Think About It." Read the theme statement below it.

- Q7 for anyone willing to share.

Day Three

- Read 4th paragraph under "Israel's identity. Read 2nd paragraph under "Let's Get Started."

- Skip Q8, but have them look at the map of the tribes.

- Q9: Look at David's line. Jesus knew He descended from David.

- Q10 and read the 2 paragraph that follow this question. Skip "Focus on the Meaning."

- Q11: Read the verses for both Sheerah and Jabez. Q12. Read first bullet point.

Day Four

- Ask what grabbed their attention from "Historical Perspective."

- Read 1 Chronicles 11:1-9. Qs13 & 14. Read "Historical Insight."

- Qs15 & 16. General discussion.

- Read 1 Chronicles 12:18, 38-40. Qs17 & 18.

- Qs19 & 20.

Other

- Discuss the podcast. Read the paragraph about identity (4th bullet after "Knowing Who You Are"). Read together the identity statement at the bottom, "I am in Christ…"

- Pray

> **Recommendation:** Listen to a worship song such as "In Christ Alone," which fits very well with this study.

LESSON 2: REJOICE IN ALL THINGS

This lesson covers several chapters. Choose ahead of time which verses from the questions the group will read aloud as you proceed through the discussion. My recommendations are below.

Start with prayer.

Day One

- Ask what grabbed their attention from the information on page 21.
- Read 1 Chronicles 13:1-4, 7-14. Ask if anyone did Q1. Summarize "Historical Insight." Q2.
- Q3. Skip "Think About It."
- Read 1 Chronicles 14:8-17. Qs4 & 5.
- Discuss Q6. Emphasize the application for today, including the "Think About It."

Day Two

- Read 1 Chronicles 15:1-4, 13-16, 16:1. Qs7-9. Skip Q10.
- Skip reading 1 Chronicles 16:4-6, 37-42. Q11. Skip "Scriptural Insight."
- Read 1 Chronicles 16:7-36 in three sections. Ask Q12 bullets for each section.
- Talk about the "Focus on the Meaning."
- Q13. Encourage the creative ones to share theirs.

Day Three

- Read 1 Chronicles 17:1-3. Ask Q14.
- Read 1 Chronicles 17:4-6 and 11-15. Ask Q15. Read "Scriptural Insight."
- Read 1 Chronicles 17:16-19, 20-24, and 25-27. Q16. Skip "Think About It."
- Q17 briefly. Don't read verses.
- Q18.

Day Four

- Don't spend time speculating about the census. Read the paragraph just before Q19.
- Qs19 & 20. Don't read the verses. Skip 'Focus on the Meaning."
- Read 1 Chronicles 21:15-19. Q 21.
- Read 1 Chronicles 21:20-22:1. Qs22 & 23. Read "Scriptural Insight."
- Qs24 & 25. Read theme statement together.

Other

- Ask for comments from podcast.
- Pray.

Recommendation: Listen to a worship song such as "You Are God Alone" by Phillips, Craig, & Dean, which fits very well with this study.

LESSON 3: THE JOY OF DELIGHTING IN GOD

This lesson covers several chapters. Choose ahead of time which verses from the questions the group will read aloud as you proceed through the discussion. My recommendations are below.

Start with prayer.

Day One

- Ask what grabbed their attention from the "Historical Perspective." Q1: Skip verses.
- Q2: Read in sections and discuss bullet points for each section.
- Q3: Read vv. 17-19. Read Scriptural Insight.
- Q4.

Day Two

- Ask who likes to organize. Skip reading verses in questions. Q5. Read "Scriptural Insight."
- Q6: Skip second bullet. Read "Focus on the Meaning."
- Q7: Read just the New Testament verses. Ask how that works in them today.
- Qs8 - 10. Read the "Scriptural Insight" and the paragraph that follows.
- Q12. Skip reading verses.

Day Three

- Q13: Skip verses. Read "Think About It."
- Qs14 & 15: Read verses.
- Q16: Skip verses. Read "Scriptural Insight."
- Q17. This can be a great sharing question.

Day Four

- Qs18 & 19: Skip verses.
- Read 1 Chronicles 29:10-20. Qs20&21. Read "Focus on the Meaning."
- Q22. Skip verses.
- Q23. Talk about praying this for family members and for the group.
- Q24. Read theme statement together.

Other

- Ask for comments from podcast.
- Pray.

> **Recommendation:** Listen to a worship song such as "Blessed Be the Name of the Lord," which fits very well with this lesson

LESSON 4: READY, SET, BUILD!

This lesson covers several chapters. Choose ahead of time which verses from the questions the group will read aloud as you proceed through the discussion. My recommendations are below.

Start with prayer.

Day One

- Q1: Read 2 Chronicles 1:7-12 and 1 Kings 3:7-9. Skip the other verses and the "Think About It."
- Q2: Read 1 Kings 4:29-34. Read "Scriptural Insight."
- Qs3 & 4.
- Q5: Read James 1:5 and 3:13-17.

Day Two

- Qs6 & 7: Skip reading verses. Find Tyre and Joppa on the map. Read "Historical Insight."
- Q8: Read 2 Chronicles 2:3-7.
- Q9: Read 2 Chronicles 2:12-14.
- Qs10 & 11: Skip verses.

Day Three

- Qs12 - 14: Read 2 Chronicles 3:1. Skip the other verses.
- Skip Q15. Read the "Historical Insight."
- Q16: Read Hebrews 8:5 and the "Historical Insight."
- Q17.

Day Four

- State the answer to Q18. Ask Qs19 & 20. Skip reading verses.
- Q21: Read 2 Chronicles 5:13-14.
- Q22: Read Exodus 13:20-22, answer question. Read Exodus 40:34-38, answer question.
- Q23: Read Acts 2:1-4, the "Historical Insight," and the paragraph that follows. Skip "Scriptural Insight."
- Q24: Read Hebrews 9:24 and 10:19-22.
- Q25. Read theme statement together.

Other

- Ask for comments about podcast.
- Pray.

Recommendation: Listen to a worship song such as "You Are God Alone" by Phillips, Craig, & Dean, which fits very well with this study.

LESSON 5: THE JOY OF GOD'S PRESENCE

This lesson covers several chapters. Choose ahead of time which verses from the questions the group will read aloud as you proceed through the discussion. My recommendations are below.

Start with prayer.

Day One

- Q1: Read 2 Chronicles 6:10-11.
- Read 2 Chronicles 6:14, 17-21. Qs2&3. Skip "Scriptural Insight."
- Q4: Skip reading verses. Quickly give answers from chart. Read "Historical Insight."
- Q5: Read vv. 32-33.
- Q6: Read 2 Chronicles 6:40-42.
- Q7.

Day Two

- Q8: Read 2 Chronicles 7:1-3. Skip paragraph that follows.
- Q9: Read 2 Chronicles 7:12-18. Read "Historical Insight" and "Think About It."
- Q10.

Day Three

- Q11: Skip reading verses.
- Q12: Read 2 Chronicles 9:1-2, 5-8. Read "Historical Insight" and "Scriptural Insight."
- Q13. If time, depending upon your group.

Day Four

- Q14: Skip reading verses. Read paragraph that follows.
- Q15: Read 1 Kings 11:4-13. Read "Scriptural Insight" that follows.
- Q16: Skip reading verses. Read and discuss "Scriptural Insight."
- Qs17 & 18.
- Read theme statement together.

Other

- Ask for comments about podcast, especially the "Choosing to Embrace or Forsake God's Presence" section.
- Pray.

Recommendation: Listen to a worship song such as "Above All," by Michael W Smith which fits very well with this lesson.

LESSON 6: THE CHOICE TO EMBRACE OR FORSAKE GOD

This lesson covers several chapters. Choose ahead of time which verses from the questions the group will read aloud as you proceed through the discussion. My recommendations are below.

Start with prayer.

Day One

- Briefly recap the "Historical Perspective." Skip the "Historical Insight."
- Q1: Read 2 Chronicles 10:6-11. Skip the "Scriptural Insight."
- Q2: Read 2 Chronicles 11:2-4..
- Q3: Read 2 Chronicles 11:13-17.
- Read the paragraph before Q4. Do Q4.

Day Two

- Q5: Skip "Historical Insight." Read 2 Chronicles 12:5-8. Read the first "Focus on the Meaning." Skip the next one.
- Q6: Read 2 Chronicles 13:4-12. Read "Scriptural Insight."
- Q7.
- Q8: Read Ephesians 2:4-10.

Day Three

- Q9: Read 2 Chronicles 14:2-5.
- Q10: Read 2 Chronicles 14:11.
- Q11: Read 2 Chronicles 15:1-2, 7-8.
- Q12: Read 2 Chronicles 15:12-15. Read "Focus on the Meaning."
- Q13: Read Acts 17:26-27.

Day Four

- Q14: Read 2 Chronicles 16:7-10. Skip the first "Focus on the Meaning" and read the second one.
- Q15 & 16. Read paragraphs after Q16.
- Qs17 & 18.
- Read theme statement together.

Other

- Ask for comments about podcast. Discuss the "Leave No Room for Excuses" section.
- Pray.

> **Recommendation:** Listen to a worship song such as "Build My Life," which fits very well with this lesson.

LESSON 7: OLD TESTAMENT DISCIPLEMAKING

This lesson covers several chapters. Choose ahead of time which verses from the questions the group will read aloud as you proceed through the discussion. My recommendations are below. Tell them ahead of time that their Q6 story should be ~1 minute or less.

Start with prayer.

Day One

- Q1: Read 2 Chronicles 17:3-6. Read the "Think About It."

- Q2: Read 2 Chronicles 17:9.

- Q3: Read 2 Chronicles 19:4-9. Read "Historical Insight."

- Qs4 & 5. Read "Becoming a disciplemaker" section.

- Q6. Spend time sharing your 3-word stories. Emphasize how they can be used.

Day Two

- Read the first sentence in the paragraph. Read the "Historical Insight." Don't read verses.

- Q7: Read paragraph. Answer first 2 bullets. Read 2 Chronicles 19:1-3. Answer last bullet.

- Q8: Don't read verses.

- Q9. Read 2 Corinthians 6:14-16. Discuss the questions. Skip "Scriptural Insight."

- Q10. Read paragraph. Discuss the "Compromise is dangerous" section. Read Isaiah 32:7. Then, answer Q10 questions.

Day Three

- Q11: Read 2 Chronicles 20:12-19 from the book. Answer questions.

- Read the "Focus on the Meaning."

- Q12: Read 2 Chronicles 20:20-22, 27-30.

- Q13: Read 2 Chronicles 20:31-33.

- Q14: Read the definition of fear and the paragraph that follows if time. Say the four truths together.

Day Four

- Skip reading passage. Q15: Read 2 Chronicles 21:7.

- Q16: Read "Scriptural Insight." Read 2 Chronicles 21:12-15.

- Q17: Skip reading verse.

- Qs18 & 19. Read theme statement together.

Other

- Podcast: Emphasize God's mercy not to define us by our mistakes (last bullet point)

- Pray.

Recommendation: Listen to a worship song such as "You Are God Alone," which fits very well with this lesson.

LESSON 8: HALF-HEARTED OBEDIENCE

This lesson covers several chapters. Choose ahead of time which verses from the questions the group will read aloud as you proceed through the discussion. My recommendations are below.

Start with prayer.

Day One

- Q1: Read 2 Chronicles 22:2-4.
- Q2. Read "Think About It."
- Q3: Read 2 Chronicles 22: 10-12. Read "Historical Insight." Skip reading Exodus 2:1-10.
- Q4. Focus on the bad influences and how to overcome them. Read Titus 2:3-5 to answer next question. Skip "Think About It."

Day Two

- Q5: Read 2 Chronicles 23:2-3. Skip "Scriptural Insight."
- Q6: Read 2 Chronicles 23:11 and Deuteronomy 17:18-19.
- Q7: Skip verses. Read "Think About It."
- Q8: Read 2 Chronicles 23:16-21.
- Q9. Talk about generational wickedness that has affected their families and examples of breaking the cycles.

Day Three

- Q10: Read 2 Chronicles 24:1-3.
- Q11: Read 2 Chronicles 24:17-22.
- Q12 and read the 2 paragraphs before Q13. Do Q13.

Day Four

- Q14: Read 2 Chronicles 25:1-4.
- Q15: Skip verses.
- Q16: Read 2 Chronicles 25:14-16.
- Q17: Skip verses. Read and discuss "Think About It."
- Q18: Skip verses. Read paragraph before Q19.
- Q19. Share examples from what they have learned.
- Q20. Read theme statement together.

Other

- Podcast: Ask for comments, especially anything related to half-heartedness.
- Pray.

> **Recommendation:** Listen to a worship song such as "I Need You" by Chris Tomlin, which fits very well with this lesson.

LESSON 9: THAT BOASTFUL PRIDE OF LIFE

This lesson covers several chapters. Choose ahead of time which verses from the questions the group will read aloud as you proceed through the discussion. My recommendations are below.

Start with prayer.

Day One

- Q1: Read 2 Chronicles 26:3-5.
- Qs2 & 3.
- Q4: Read 2 Chronicles 26:9-10, 15. Read "Focus on the Meaning."
- Q5.

Day Two

- Q6: Read paragraph then read 2 Chronicles 26:16-20.
- Q7. Skip "Historical Insight."
- Qs8 & 9: Skip reading verses.
- Q10: Skip verses. Read "Historical Insight."
- Q11: Read 1 John 2:16 and paragraph that follows. Discuss questions.

Day Three

- Q12: Read 2 Chronicles 27:1-2, 6.
- Q13. Read "Scriptural Insight."
- Q14.
- Q15: Read 1 Corinthians 10:6-13. Discuss the questions.

Day Four

- Read 2 Chronicles 28:1-5 and paragraph before Q16.
- Qs16 & 17.
- Q 18: Read Isaiah 7:2-4, 10-14
- Qs19 – 21: Skip verses. Read paragraph after Q21. Skip "From the Hebrew" if short on time.
- Qs22 & 23 Read theme statement together.

Other

- Podcast: Ask for comments about reliance on God to overcome pride.
- Pray.

Recommendation: Listen to a worship song such as "Build My Life," which fits very well with this lesson.

LESSON 10: THE UNSTOPPABLE POWER OF GOD'S FORGIVENESS

This lesson covers several chapters. Choose ahead of time which verses from the questions the group will read aloud as you proceed through the discussion. My recommendations are below.

Start with prayer.

Day One

- Recap what was happening from the first couple of paragraphs.
- Q1: Read 2 Chronicles 29:1-5, 9-11. Read "From the Hebrew," "Think About It," and "Scriptural Insight."
- Q2: Read 2 Chronicles 29:25-31, 34-36.
- Q3

Day Two

- Q4: Skip "Focus on the Meaning." Read 2 Chronicles 30:1, 6-12. Skip "Historical Insight."
- Q5: Read 2 Chronicles 30:17-20, 25-27. Read "Think About It" and "Scriptural Insight."
- Q6: Read 2 Chronicles 31:1. Skip Q7.
- Q8: Read 2 Chronicles 31:20-21.
- Q9: Skip "Think About It."

Day Three

- Q10: Skip "Historical Insight." Read 2 Chronicles 32:1, 7-8.
- Q11: Skip reading verses.
- Q12: Read Isaiah 37:1-2, 14-20.
- Q13: Read 2 Chronicles 32:24-26. Skip Q14.
- Read paragraphs about 2 aspects of trusting God. Q15 and read "Think About It."

Day Four

- Q16: Skip reading verses and "Scriptural Insight."
- Qs17&18: Read 2 Chronicles 33:10-13, 16-17. Read "Focus on the Meaning."
- Q19
- Q20 is a tool to use. Q21. Read theme statement together.

Other

- Podcast: Discuss the gift of fear. God uses this gift to get our attention, especially when it comes to consequences for disobedience and rebellion. Ask for other comments.
- Pray.

> **Recommendation:** Listen to a worship song such as "You Are God Alone," which fits very well with this lesson.

LESSON 11: A HOPE AND A FUTURE

This lesson covers several chapters. Choose ahead of time which verses from the questions the group will read aloud as you proceed through the discussion. My recommendations are below.

Start with prayer.

Day One

- Q1: Read 2 Chronicles 34:1-5. Skip "Think About It."
- Q2: State the answer. Skip the "Historical Insight."
- Q3: Read 2 Chronicles 34:22-28. Read "Focus on the Meaning."
- Q4: Don't read verses.
- Q5.

Day Two

- Q6: Read 2 Chronicles 35:1-4. Read "Scriptural Insight."
- Qs7&8: Read 2 Chronicles 35: 20-26. Skip "Think About it."
- Qs9&10. Read paragraph after Q10.
- Q11.

Day Three

- Q12: Don't read the verses. Look at the chart to see those continuing David's line.
- Skip Q13. Q14: Read 2 Chronicles 36:15-21. Read "Scriptural Insight."
- Q15: Read Jeremiah 25:8-12; 27:22. Read "Historical Insight."
- Skip Q16. Q17: Read Jeremiah 29:4-14. Read "Focus on the Meaning."
- Q18.

Day Four

- Read the two paragraphs before Q19.
- Q19: Read 2 Chronicles 36:21-23.
- Read Ezra 1:2-4 and "Scriptural Insight." Qs20 & 21.
- Q22-24: Don't read verses. Put names in the chart.
- Q25: Read Ezra 3:1-2. Read the paragraphs that follow.
- Qs26 & 27. Read theme statement together.

Other

- Podcast: Draw out highlights from "God's Steadfast Love Planned for the Future" section.
- Pray.

Recommendation: Listen to a worship song such as "Lord, I Need You," which fits very well with this lesson.

Sources

The following resources were used in the preparation and writing of this study.

1. Chuck Swindoll, *First Chronicles Overview,* www.insight.org, accessed 10/19/19

2. Chuck Swindoll, *Second Chronicles Overview*, www.insight.org, accessed 10/19/19

3. Cory Asbury, "Reckless Love of God"

4. "Create Your Own 3-Word Testimony!" accessed at www.evantell.org

5. Dr. J. Vernon McGee, *Notes & Outlines 1 & 2 Chronicles*

6. Dr. Tom Constable, *Dr. Constable's Notes on 1 Chronicles 2019 Edition*

7. Dr. Tom Constable, *Dr. Constable's Notes on 2 Chronicles 2019 Edition*

8. John F. Walvoord and Roy B. Zuck, *The Bible Knowledge Commentary Old Testament,* Victor Books, 1983.

9. Map 49, "The Boundaries of the Twelve Tribes," www.thebiblejourney.org

10. Steven J. Cole, "The Seduction of Success (2 Chronicles 26)," www.Bible.org, accessed 10/29/19

11. The *NIV Study Bible New International Version*, Zondervan Bible Publishers, 1985.

12. *The Kingdoms of Israel and Judah map 1994 version,* www.bible.ca, accessed from www.paradisepbc.org 10/25/19

13. *Timeline: Prophets in the Reigns of Kings of Judah and Israel,* www.miketaylor.org, accessed 10/1/19

14. Tim Stevenson, sermon notes, "Faith Encounters" Series

15. "What is the purpose of First and Second Chronicles?" www.gotquestions.org, accessed 10/29/19

16. "What happened to the lost tribes of Israel?" www.gotquestions.org, accessed 1/09/2020.

17. "Who is a Jews?" www.jewfaq.org, accessed 1/17/2020.

18. "Why Study the Books of 1-2 Chronicles?" James Duguid, www.crossway.org, written June 18, 2018, accessed 10/13/2019.